# MEDICAL
# DEVICE
# COMPANY
## IN A BOX

Published by Advantage, Charleston, South Carolina.
Member of Advantage Media Group.

ADVANTAGE is a registered trademark, and the Advantage colophon is a trademark of Advantage Media Group, Inc.

Printed in the United States of America.

10  9  8  7  6  5  4  3  2  1

ISBN: 978-1-59932-861-4
LCCN: 2017950360

Cover design by Katie Biondo.
Layout design by Megan Elger.

This publication is designed to provide accurate and authoritative information in regard to the subject matter covered. It is sold with the understanding that the publisher is not engaged in rendering legal, accounting, or other professional services. If legal advice or other expert assistance is required, the services of a competent professional person should be sought.

Advantage Media Group is proud to be a part of the Tree Neutral® program. Tree Neutral offsets the number of trees consumed in the production and printing of this book by taking proactive steps such as planting trees in direct proportion to the number of trees used to print books. To learn more about Tree Neutral, please visit **www.treeneutral.com.**

Advantage Media Group is a publisher of business, self-improvement, and professional development books. We help entrepreneurs, business leaders, and professionals share their Stories, Passion, and Knowledge to help others Learn & Grow. Do you have a manuscript or book idea that you would like us to consider for publishing? Please visit advantagefamily.com or call **1.866.775.1696.**

THE CASE FOR CONSILISO

# MEDICAL DEVICE COMPANY

## IN A BOX

MARK RUTKIEWICZ

*Advantage*®

*To Joe and Caroline.*

# TABLE OF CONTENTS

# FOREWORD

Mark and I worked together for several years at AGA Medical. This collaboration was important, since I was in Regulatory Affairs and he was in Quality. That partnership is a vital one for a medical device company. In addition, because we developed primarily structural heart-implant devices, we were working in an industry heavily scrutinized by regulators and requiring a high degree of quality and control for the patients we served. This certainly tested the concepts Mark developed, which have become Consiliso.

If you take a big step back and not focus only on Quality Systems, we all have a daily routine we develop in our work lives. These are based on our priorities, deliverables, interactions with colleagues, our skills and experiences, and the cultural framework of an organization. Whenever we view part of our workday as a separate process, we struggle to incorporate that into our daily routine. This can cause us to make mistakes or slow down, since it is outside of our normal daily activities.

Now, think about that example in relationship to Quality Systems. There are organizations where Quality System tools, procedures, and processes are entirely separate from our routine workday and other business processes. A common symptom of this is having repeat Corrective and Preventive Actions (CAPAs) for individuals in a company for not following a procedure. I think we all see this from time to time. However, it can be a red flag that following procedures might be outside of their normal workday processes, which is bound to cause errors.

If you imagine a system where the Quality System and other business processes are one fluid system that align and become essentially one business process, that's what Mark imagined as well. He took it a step further and assembled the building blocks for us to use. It was amazing to see how functions like research, marketing, and legal also embraced these concepts.

I had the opportunity to see this system in action at AGA Medical with Mark. For example, we worked closely with our Operations and Production teams to make all our product, regulatory, and clinical processes integrated, which reduced errors and made the Quality System a part of our daily lives, not a separate requirement to fulfill. Not only is that truly fulfilling the spirit of Quality System regulations around the globe, but it makes our daily work focused, aligned across the business, and simpler to understand. I congratulate Mark on creating such a thoughtful and useful tool for all of us!

Amanda M. Johnson
Vice President, Regulatory and Medical Affairs
Spectranetics Corporation

# ACKNOWLEDGMENTS

I would like to thank John Ledy and Dave Jessen for their support in bringing this book and Consiliso to life.

I would also like to thank Tim Brown for all his insights in developing Consiliso technical concepts.

Lastly, I want to thank Wendy Stone for challenging me in developing the Consiliso processes, editing the books, and encouraging me in this massive endeavor.

# ABOUT THE AUTHOR

Mark Rutkiewicz is Vice President of Quality at Innovize, a contract manufacturer for the medical device industry. Mark holds a bachelor's degree in electrical engineering from the University of Minnesota and a master's degree in applied liberal studies from Hamline University in St. Paul, Minnesota. He is a Kellogg Executive Scholar, holds Configuration Management II certification from the Institute of Configuration Management, and is certified as a Professional Engineer by the Minnesota Board of Engineering (Board of AELSLAGID). Mark's expertise in the medical device industry includes managing all areas of product development, quality control, regulatory oversight, operations, and information management activities for Class I, II, and III implantable and non-implantable medical devices. In each of his positions, he built and rebuilt online, integrated, corporation-wide, quality information systems.

Mark has also developed and configured electronic, disposable, capital, consumer, and software products. He is currently involved in the Case for Quality project of the Medical Device Innovation Consortium (MDIC), and previously served as the industry representative on the FDA's Ear, Nose, and Throat (ENT) Devices Panel. Mark used his thirty years of experience in the medical device industry to develop Consiliso, which provides the means for all medical device companies to properly design their business processes.

# IMAGINE A BETTER WAY

Whatever the size or scope of your medical device company—start-up, small but growing, or multinational corporation—one aspect of your business is constant: In order to achieve approvals and pass regulatory inspections, you must have a compliant *Quality System*.

To consistently create high-quality products, that Quality System must be robust: It must capture all required documentation and the key metrics needed to improve performance.

Too often, however, as a company matures, its Quality System becomes fractured into different silos of information owned by various departments. Rarely is a company forward-thinking enough to leverage its Quality System technologies and processes to handle all the other regulated aspects of the business: clinical trials, environmental, health and safety, and financial processes.

Information silos happen even in the smallest of companies. I saw it when working with a two-person company that produced a two-sided product with printing on one side, adhesive on the other. The instructions were difficult to interpret, so each of the two individuals in the company was approached separately for clarification, only to find out that each one had a different understanding of what the product actually entailed. If that happens in a company of two people, imagine how many times a similar situation happens in a company of three thousand people—and at what cost and what impact to quality and time? **Consiliso**, the system I'm discussing in this book, ensures everyone is on the same page, for all business processes.

As the leader of a company, you know that the information generated by business activities is vital for decision-making. However, if your people don't have easy access to that information, if the collection of data is inconsistent, or if it takes days (or weeks!) to find all the data to create a report, it becomes difficult for your leadership to improve the process or see where additional attention is needed.

There is a better way.

Imagine having an integrated system that immediately lets you see whether you are hitting your key performance indicator (KPI) metrics and that also gathers those metrics in a highly efficient manner—a system that allows you to do a "deep dive" into more detailed information. Imagine that system being a natural part of the way in which your people do their work. And, you wouldn't need another latest-and-greatest software application to make it all happen.

Establishing and maintaining documented control of a myriad of activities—product development, design, manufacturing processes, supply chain, distribution, training, complaint processing, adverse-event reporting, and so much more—is essential. But in companies of any size, too often these activities are cumbersome and inefficient, no matter the technologies used to support the business.

A good indicator of how well your Quality System functions is to ask your engineers a few simple questions: In order to make a simple change to a manufacturing process step, how many hours do you spend on the entire process? How many meetings must you call? And how long does it take to obtain the approval process through the change order (CO) procedure? If their answer is that it requires more than a few days from the time they have determined what change should be made to the time that change is implemented on the floor, then you have a serious problem.

The problem is *not* an overly burdensome regulatory environment. A system meant to ensure patient safety is a good thing for everyone, but if poorly designed, executed, and maintained, it hamstrings efforts to identify and analyze problems and to improve the product accordingly.

**The problem is *not* an overly burdensome regulatory environment.**

Still, most medical device companies build their Quality Systems in an organic, piecemeal fashion, often in response to their interpretation of specific regulations and standards. Regulators, however, desire companies to analyze all their activities and how those activities adversely affect product quality and efficacy.

In other words, regulators want you to design quality into your *processes*. The problem is no one has, before Consiliso, been taught exactly how to do that.

The ISO Quality System standards define a *process approach*. That definition requires you to identify and determine the interactions of your business processes. It does require you to design your processes to work efficiently, but the design of Consiliso achieves both compliance and efficiency.

**Regulators want you to design quality into your *processes*. The problem is no one has, before Consiliso, been taught exactly how to do that.**

For example, the most common mistake medical device companies make is having a document-centric rather than part-centric system. This approach limits their ability to control processes. Yes, you need documents, but they must be linked to part objects (i.e., virtual representations of physical things), which is a natural outcome of a well-designed process to *build a better product* than your competitors. This is a prime example of what regulatory bodies mean when they advise companies to design processes to achieve compliance.

## A SHIFT IN THINKING AND A BLUEPRINT FOR DOING

Consiliso is fundamentally different from traditional process- or business-improvement programs. In fact, many people refer to it as a "medical device company in a box." With Consiliso-level thinking, you understand that a problem is a problem: No matter where it originates or who deals with it, the business process is the same. For instance, if you have a computer system properly designed to handle *problems*, the only difference between the *where* and the *who* is the categorization data (metadata) for the type of problem and the workflow routing for who analyzes and works toward a resolution.

Consiliso shows, in detail, *how* to properly design *all* your business processes (not just your Quality System). The Latin word *consili* means "design," and the Greek word *isos* means "equal." Therefore, *Consiliso* means designing for equality and unity of processes and standards.

The power of the Consiliso approach involves altering your perception of how your company runs. It's critical for you to develop an eye for the unity of *processes* across different departments, functions, or activities. If nothing else, that shift in thinking leads you to redesign your processes to reduce duplication, integrate information so it may be easily accessed and analyzed by everyone who performs related work, leverage existing technologies and best practices, and create other efficiencies and improvements.

To attain both compliance and a competitive edge, you must expend some effort to design your quality processes with the same expertise you bring to the table when determining how to build your product. You must *engineer* it for efficiency, flexibility, and usability. If that sounds like an enormous undertaking, rest assured that the majority of the work is already done. Consiliso contains all the information required to establish, across your company, these world-class processes that have been carefully designed, developed, and implemented in a variety of different sizes and types of medical device companies over decades.

I wrote this book to give you an overview of the methods involved in employing Consiliso in your medical device company. The chapters ahead also provide specific examples of how Consiliso has helped companies develop world-class products without becoming overburdened by compliance requirements.

## BEEN THERE, DONE THAT

How do I know what I know about medical device companies? I've been in the medical device industry for thirty years. That includes leadership positions at a half dozen different medical device companies where I've built or rebuilt the entire quality, regulatory, clinical, financial, and environmental business systems, essentially changing the fundamental aspects of how the company performed its work.

As an electrical engineer by training, I solve problems from a systems-engineering point of view for companies large and small. But I also have a master's degree in applied liberal studies with a business leadership focus. While my engineering training taught me to view problem resolution from a mechanistic perspective, my leadership training taught me to look at the human side of every equation.

Having been a business executive, engineer, and quality/compliance professional, I've learned a great deal over the years about the needs and wants of each of these roles in a medical device company and how each of these roles integrates with the others. I see connectedness and patterns that others miss, and I am experienced in mapping out the interaction of the various processes.

Based on my experiences, I developed Consiliso, a concept that works for all medical device companies. While easily implemented in smaller companies, the system is capable of scaling up to the largest multinational corporation.

In the chapters ahead, I'll share more insights to help you see the value of Consiliso.

- Chapter 1 explains Consiliso.

- Chapter 2 defines how companies create business processes and how those work with Consiliso.

- Chapter 3 discusses managing your company to produce safe products.

- Chapter 4 explains how Consiliso improves managing the life cycle of human clinical trials.

- Chapter 5 illustrates how Consiliso improves your financial controls and reporting to prevent fraud and ensure accurate data.

- Chapter 6 defines the seven core business processes needed for every company.

- Chapter 7 explains how Consiliso simplifies audits and increases productivity.

## CONSILISO—BUSINESS SYSTEMS, BUSINESS PROCESSES, PEOPLE

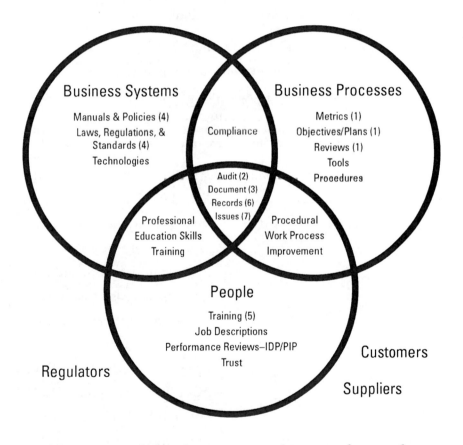

Implementation of Consiliso integrates three core frames of every company: business systems, business processes, and people.

- **Business systems** are driven by standards and requirements-management processes, one of seven core business processes of Consiliso. The "business systems" frame defines your high-level business operating manuals and policies along with applicable laws, regulations, and standards.

- **Business processes** are driven by management processes, another core process. The "business processes" frame involves metrics, objectives/plans, and reviews, and it is supported by tools and procedures.

- **People** are driven by another core process, the training process, with support from your human resources processes through job descriptions, performance reviews, individual development plans (IDP), performance improvement plans, (PIP), and the culture of trust in your company.

In the center of the graphic where the three frames intersect, the four other core processes occur: audits, documents, records, and issues. In other words, it takes involvement from business systems, business processes, and people to deal with auditing, documentation, records, and issues management. Chapter 6, "Seven Core Processes," provides more specifics about Consiliso's core processes. All of the other business processes in your company need to occur where the three frames intersect.

It takes involvement from business systems, business processes, and people to deal with auditing, documentation, records, and issues management.

The graphic shows that where business processes and people intersect, procedural work and business processes improvements are involved. Compliance comes into play when a business process overlaps with a business system. Compliance, of course, involves ensuring you are following the rules and regulations. And, where people and business systems connect, professional education and skills training comes into play.

## LEVEL E – REACTIVE/FIREFIGHTING

Before implementing Consiliso, the three frames of a company that tie into Consiliso—business systems, business processes, and people—are barely connected. Essentially, they exist independently.

When these three areas of a company lack integration, the company usually operates in a reactive, or firefighting, mode. No one really knows what anyone else is doing until a fire erupts. Then, there you are, spending time, money, and other resources trying to douse the flames. There are five modes, or levels:

- Level E – Reactive/Firefighting
- Level D – Maintain with Tribal Knowledge
- Level C – Project to Improve
- Level B – Lean/VOC/Scrum
- Level A – Proactive/Consiliso

## LEVEL D – MAINTAIN WITH TRIBAL KNOWLEDGE

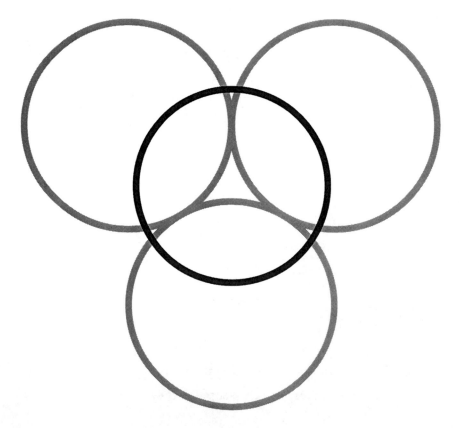

Consiliso, the darker circle, when initially implemented, provides that integration. It starts bringing all the areas together. The company begins to maintain control with the integration of tribal knowledge, a concept I'll talk more about in Chapter 2, "Your Business Systems: Then and Now."

## LEVEL C – PROJECT TO IMPROVE

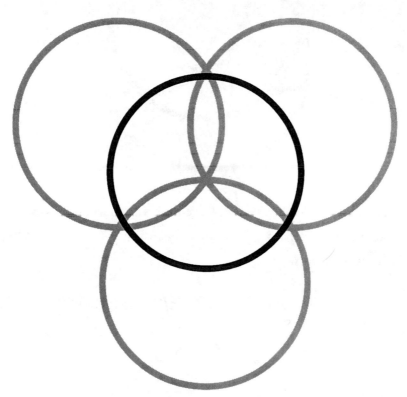

With the addition of more Consiliso features, more integration occurs. Projects improve as more areas of the company become tightly connected.

## LEVEL B – LEAN/VOC/SCRUM

As more of Consiliso is implemented, a higher level of integration allows the company to employ *Lean*, *Voice of Customer* (VOC), and *Scrum* concepts.

## LEVEL A – PROACTIVE/CONSILISO

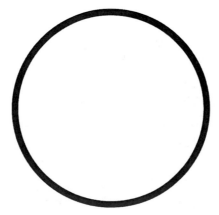

With Consiliso implemented, the three frames of the company become fully integrated, and the company moves from a reactive to a proactive mode.

## A NEW PERSPECTIVE

Consiliso is a methodology for using a systems engineering approach to business processes. Take it from me: It's never too late to learn a better way to do business. I discovered that truth after being in the industry for a few years and reaching a leadership position in the documentation area for a large medical device company. I was managing product configurations for some time, and my group of about fifty people needed more training in the configuration management process. I approved the three-week training course for the team, but then one of my leads told me, "You need it too, Mark." I thought he was crazy since I could probably teach the class. But I agreed to take the training as a student to ensure that everyone— myself included—was on the same page. Turned out we had a great instructor, and I learned more about not only the parts of the process that I already knew, but I also discovered how configuration management connected everything together. I ultimately used similar concepts to add another dimension to Consiliso, allowing control and reuse of master information across the business systems.

I wrote this book to help executives, investors, regulatory bodies, and management in the medical device industry better understand Consiliso. I want to convince you—through using real-world examples instead of theory—that your medical device company needs to engineer and integrate its business processes. And, in using Consiliso to do so, you will speed up your product development while achieving compliance with maximum efficiency and quality.

Before reading this book, you may be wondering how you, as a medical device executive bombarded with approaches by a variety of methodologies and ideas, actually *apply* Consiliso concepts in your company. Does using Consiliso mean that you, yourself, need to have an engineering background? Absolutely not. What I want to achieve in writing this book is to help you shift your perspective to lead the effort to become the chief architect of your own company's processes. I wrote this book for you.

For analysts and engineers, managers running departments, and IT people setting up the supporting technologies, I also wrote an exhaustively detailed textbook on *how* to specifically do what I have done (design processes). As chief architect, you simply need to provide guidance to your people on how to adapt this detailed blueprint to your company's specific needs, such as deciding which elective business processes apply. You may download or purchase a hard copy of the textbook at Consiliso.com.

In addition to the experiences in the medical device industry that I've already shared with you, I'm going to provide more experiences in the pages ahead. In these stories, I've changed the names or altered minor details to protect the privacy of companies involved.

Read on to learn more about how Consiliso can integrate all aspects of your medical device company and make it a world-class business, no matter its size or the complexity of your products.

# CHAPTER 1

# CONSILISO: WHAT IT IS, WHAT IT MEANS TO YOU

Inspections and audits are "a necessary evil" for medical device makers. They are the oversight that ensures a company is complying with a plethora of regulations. If a US Food and Drug Administration (FDA) inspection or audit turns up issues, you will spend the next few days responding to their Form-483 (483) findings. If the inspection revealed systemic issues and your response simply states that you will fix those specific issues and follow up with the training of personnel, guess what? The problem will likely escalate to the next level. A warning letter is probably in your future.

That and more happened when I was working at a Class III implantable device company. We had issues from a recall that led to multiple 483s from multiple inspections. Those led to an FDA warning letter, which finally escalated to a consent decree. That consent decree, of course, allowed the FDA to come in pretty much whenever it chose to inspect the company.

When dealing with those FDA findings, I remember sitting in meetings with groups of people who, half the time, did not even understand the regulations and standards they were expected to meet. When those in management read the regulation or standard, they immediately applied its internal design interpretation, showing that managers could not separate the requirements (*what*) from the design (*how*).

In response to the consent decree, the company's CEO beefed up the internal audit group and had every functional area resolve the issues that had arisen from the FDA inspections.

Not surprisingly, the subsequent in-depth internal audit still found huge holes in meeting the FDA requirements. The main reason? The Quality System, theoretically designed to apply every applicable regulation and standard, was built in parts and pieces. That meant the system was made up of multiple procedures owned by different departments that defined how they each did their work but not how the *process* worked. Many duplicate and conflicting procedures existed. For example, the company had eight corrective action processes when it only needed one. We also found two procedures for controlling lab notebooks and a half dozen ways to release documents.

Ultimately, the company determined that many of the problems were within the Quality department, so the CEO created a compliance group under the Legal department to initiate business system changes. The compliance group's major responsibility was to track whether the regulations and standards changed or if regulatory body interpretation drifted over time. The compliance group's goal was to create a set of corporate compliance requirements that combined all the regulations and Quality System standards into what was required, not how they must be implemented. Experts/management in the functional areas affected helped develop these requirements, and they were validated by outside experts.

With those issues resolved, I then came up with some design concepts to change the business processes and business systems, along with the procedures for the entire company. With those concepts, we redesigned the entire Quality System. We "rewired the house with the electricity on" (a phrase coined by one of my former bosses); we changed out all the processes and procedures while the company was still operating. Once we had the new Quality System in place, the company managed to undergo twenty-seven FDA inspections over the next three years with only one 483 finding.

## KNOW THE DIFFERENCE: REQUIREMENTS VERSUS DESIGN

That experience in dealing with the FDA was an early revelation for me in recognizing that many manufacturers have trouble discerning the difference between requirements (the *what*) and design (the *how*).

Early in my career, I also had trouble understanding the difference in these concepts. But I was fortunate to have a coworker take the time to explain them to me. That happened when I was assigned to a new product development team. It was my third role at the company after having worked in supplier development and then in manufacturing.

In 1996, the FDA's Quality System Regulation (QSR) required companies to document their product design requirements, but I did not know the difference between requirements and design. On the software side, the concept of design requirements was well understood. The software needed to perform a specific function: requirements described the function; design was the actual software code. On the other hand, being an electrical engineer, I was more accustomed to only seeing the concept of design in the form of a drawing. It took many hours of explanation by a software engineer on our team to help me understand the differences.

As it applies to medical devices, a requirement is *what* a medical device is supposed to do, while a design is the *description* of the physical characteristics of what is delivered.

---

Using an example of something simple like a tongue depressor, what is its requirement?

- It is used to push the tongue down. *Wrong.* That description is not specific enough.

- It is made of a six-inch piece of wood. *Wrong.* That is too specific and involves design.

- It must be able to reach the entire length of a human tongue. *Okay.* That works as a requirement.

- It needs to be made of wood. *Wrong.* That is design, not requirement.

- It needs to be made of something that is compatible with the human mouth. *Wrong.* That is not specific enough for a medical device.

- It must have round ends. *Wrong.* That is design.

- It must not damage the patient's mucosal surfaces when used to examine the mouth cavity. *Okay.*

- It needs to be biologically compatible per ISO 10993 for less than twenty-four hours' duration of surface mucosal contact. *Yes!* Now you are beginning to get it.

That requirement determined, a design statement would then be:

- The device is: 6 inches long, 3/4-inch wide, with 3/8-inch radius ends, and made of 1/16-inch-thick pine wood, sanded smooth so there are no sharp edges or splinters.

---

Designs are verified on the production floor by test and inspection. Requirements are validated by the user or in a simulated user environment.

Standards and requirements of many kinds apply to medical device companies, including product-specific, project-specific, internal company, industry, regulatory body, and internationally accepted. All the different types of standard, definition, and management methods make confusion, duplication, and failure to achieve real consensus on what applies seem inevitable. Consiliso, however, provides a consistent way to identify, control, and link all your applicable requirements.

## A LESSON IN DOCUMENTING REQUIREMENTS

Having a system that lets anyone working on a project easily access the standards and requirements documents can eliminate waste and save your company money. Let me share with you how having a way to control and link design requirements saved a company money.

While working at a small company, I needed to find a way to measure the movement of the ossicular chain (middle ear bones) during ear surgery. A laser Doppler vibrometer by itself did not do the trick because the signal was too weak, since the ossicular bones did not sufficiently reflect the laser beam. I was tasked to come up with an accessory measurement device to be used during surgery.

I thought I knew the product requirements, and since they were so simple—sterility, biocompatibility for less than twenty-four hours of exposure, and the ability to reflect the laser beam—I did not write them into a design-requirements document, which also meant there was no cross-functional review.

I found two materials that worked: one had a thin film of aluminum, and the other was a polymer with reflective properties. Aluminum may have caused issues in the biocompatible test, so I chose the polymer material. I built and sent test samples for biocompatibility and sterilization testing, and it passed. I then showed the new reflector to our clinical trial sponsor, and he conducted a lab test. The material failed the test because when fluid came in contact with the reflector during the surgical procedure, it lost all reflective properties.

I had wasted several thousands of dollars and two months of time because I did not document, review, and validate the requirements with the users and the other engineers. The other reflector with aluminum film was ultimately built, passed all tests, and worked perfectly during the procedure.

For me, and for the company, the reflector fail was a tough lesson to learn about documenting even the simplest of requirements. The Consiliso processes and tools would have given me the ability to easily find, use, and change standards and requirements, and to help eliminate wasted efforts. Consiliso also helps eliminate the risk of noncompliance when regulations change, as is the case with the new revision of the medical device Quality System standard, ISO 13485:2016, which adds significant requirements in terms of mitigating risk.

Consiliso helps mitigate risk in your organization by eliminating noncompliance when regulations change.

Having developed that basic understanding of design versus requirements early in my career, I began to connect the pieces and build what ultimately became Consiliso. Understanding the difference between design and requirements is imperative when implementing Consiliso across your company. What lies between design and requirements are your business processes, which I'll talk more about in the chapters ahead.

> **Consiliso helps mitigate risk in your organization by eliminating noncompliance when regulations change.**

The ability of the management team to understand the difference between requirements and design drives the maturity level of the company.

## CAPTURING KNOWLEDGE AS YOUR COMPANY EVOLVES

Companies are living organisms. They evolve over time. They are born, grow, merge, divest, and die. Evolution makes them mature or juvenile. Internal and external factors also affect the evolution of a company. External stakeholders can kill the company, keep it from growing, or help it grow. The management team needs to understand the motivation of the external stakeholders in order to combat or leverage that energy.

The maturity level of a company is based on its business processes: their capability, scalability, and integration. Companies must perform their activities through documented and optimized business processes instead of through a command-and-control structure. Old-fashioned command and control cannot manage complex business systems with thousands of moving parts. That structure is only as good as the knowledge of individual leaders, while a process-controlled structure contains the knowledge of thousands of experts.

Many of the Consiliso concepts are implemented independently of engaging the whole company, but they do not achieve their full effect until all the business processes freely interact. That does not mean that everyone accesses all information, but there is appropriate transparency in every business process, and the decisions the company makes are consistent with its stated goals and objectives.

For instance, if one person in your company manages a great deal of information, that individual knows where everything is. Once you add a second person to the equation—someone else sharing the information—the system becomes inefficient. That's when duplications and redundancies occur; that's when you need Consiliso.

Here's an example of how stone-simple inefficiencies cause a great amount of waste: One small company had a software engineer who worked alone and was far more productive than entire departments of software engineers at other medical device companies. Why was one person more efficient than multiple people in the same role? Because when only one person occupies a role, all the information is in that person's head. Efficiency is an integral part of the system because that lone employee doesn't need to communicate with anyone else about the work that needs to be done.

Consiliso is about understanding what kinds of information and knowledge to capture in your company, the majority of which isn't regulation-required knowledge; it is knowledge your company must maintain and use. Documentation lets you capture information in your company, and the ability to easily find and control all of that documentation gives your company a competitive advantage. What is your definition of documentation? Is it the activities of your documentation group prior to releasing documents for the production floor? Is it any controlled document? Or is it any document that gets signed? Documentation is, simply, *all* of the information needed to run your business, in whatever form is the most appropriate and efficient.

Once captured, that information must be readily available to everyone who needs it. That access helps mitigate risk and breaks down information silos. The need to show control is another aspect of the concept of open access, or transparency. So, Consiliso requires your documentation control tool to have an easy-to-use audit trail feature that records when anyone has viewed a document. The ability for anyone to see what others access provides a layer of transparency and a sense of individual responsibility.

## CONSILISO-LEVEL THINKING

As I mentioned in the book's Introduction, Consiliso is fundamentally different from traditional process-improvement or business-improvement programs because it is designed specifically for medical device manufacturers.

I created Consiliso after working in the medical device industry for thirty years, much of that time spent in leadership positions with various kinds of medical device makers. In these roles as business executive, engineer, and quality/compliance professional, I've built or rebuilt entire quality business systems that fundamentally changed how a particular company performed its work.

My educational background allows me to see both the technical and people sides of a problem. From that viewpoint, I've discovered how various roles in a company integrate with each other. I'm an architect of sorts for medical device business systems: I see the patterns and design blueprints that connect all the areas of a business. I developed Consiliso based on that concept.

**Since it is so comprehensive in the way it integrates processes, some people refer to it as a "medical device company in a box."**

Consiliso goes beyond Quality System design to include *how* to properly design *all* your business processes. Since it is so comprehensive in the way it integrates processes, some people refer to it as a "medical device company in a box."

The power of Consiliso-level thinking is in altering your perception of how your company runs. Once you develop an eye for the unity of the *processes* across different functions or activities, you begin to see how to redesign your processes toward leveraging existing data, technologies, and best practices. You discover ways to reduce duplication and integrate information so that it is easily accessed and analyzed by anyone who performs related work. This shift in perception inherently promotes creating other efficiencies and improvements across all areas of your company.

With a little effort, Consiliso enables you to design your Quality System processes with the same expertise used in building your products. It also enables you to engineer products with efficiency, flexibility, and usability, giving you an edge on both compliance and the competition.

Implementing Consiliso starts with an assessment of your current operations, and then includes a **five-phase implementation plan** with these components:

- **Step 1: Definition**. Organize and assess laws, regulations, guidelines, and standards for usage.

- **Step 2: Requirements**. Create a common set of compliance requirements based on interpretations of data from Step 1.

- **Step 3: Integration**. Design business processes and procedures in support of the requirements, and then assess your current situation and prioritize the changes.

- **Step 4: Training**. Train personnel in the requirements, business processes, and procedures that apply to their job(s).

- **Step 5: Auditing and Reporting**. Audit business processes and procedures to the requirements to assess compliance, and then report on the status.

The five-phase process is based on the plan-do-check-act (PDCA) circle developed by workplace quality and efficiency guru W. Edward Deming, and is a very simple description of an extremely complex change. That kind of change, as I mentioned earlier, is like "rewiring the house with the electricity on." It needs to be done, but doing so may give you quite a shock. The Consiliso textbook—available for hard-copy purchase at Consiliso.com—goes into greater detail, including administrative steps for undergoing such an extensive change.

## FROM REACTIVE/INEFFICIENT TO PROACTIVE/EFFICIENT

Fundamentally, Consiliso is about being proactive and efficient versus being reactive and inefficient. When companies start out, they often operate inefficiently. They are in a reactive mode, constantly putting out fires. As they mature, they become more proactive to keep fires from starting in the first place.

> **When companies start out, they often operate inefficiently. They are in a reactive mode, constantly putting out fires. As they mature, they become more proactive to keep fires from starting in the first place.**

I've designed a two-dimensional chart to demonstrate the levels of maturity and compliance a company progresses through (see Figure 1-1). *Webster's Third New International Dictionary* has eight definitions for *quality*. Two are used when dealing with business Quality Systems: a degree of excellence and a degree of conformance to a standard. The two definitions of quality represent the two axes of the chart. However, I also expanded and modified them to align with the requirements for medical device companies and the definitions for quality as formulated by Deming and another workplace quality and efficiency guru, Joseph Juran.

The Y-axis of the Maturity and Compliance Matrix represents continuous improvement. Continuous improvement is about degrees of excellence and includes:

- constant improvement of every process involved in planning, production, and service (Deming);

- making the product better by finding and resolving issues in development and in production; and

- making the processes, procedures, and tools people use better (Lean).

The X-axis represents compliance with requirements. Compliance with requirements is about the degree of conformance to a standard and includes:

- fitness for intended use (Juran);

- meeting all applicable regulations and standards (Quality System); and

- complying with the regulations and directives for all countries in which a product is sold to ensure every single product is safe and effective.

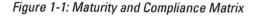

Figure 1-1: Maturity and Compliance Matrix

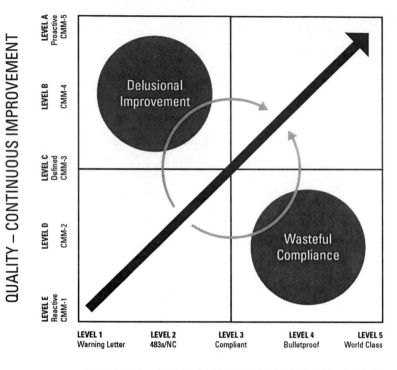

## THE Y-AXIS: CONTINUOUS IMPROVEMENT

The Y-axis is based on the company's willingness to make improvements. On the Y-axis, a company measures its progress as it changes from reactive to proactive operations. Let me break it down for you.

**Level E.** When a company first starts making a product, it doesn't have procedures; it doesn't understand the requirements. It's down in the lower left of the X/Y-axis in a reactive state. It's just solving whatever problems it can as they arise. Across the company, people are just doing what they are told; there is no real planning; people are just dealing with issues without really managing anything.

If someone leaves the company, the knowledge goes too, because nothing is written down.

**Level D**. Next, the company begins defining processes, maybe using what it has always used. Perhaps there's a hint of planning, such as a checklist used when a new employee starts with the company. Some procedures and instructions are written down so that if a member of the team leaves, operations can continue.

**Level C**. Now the company has processes, and it begins to look at whether they actually work, can be improved, or perhaps used when a new product is added to the company's offerings.

For instance, let's say the first product the company makes is a catheter that uses tubing. By level C, the company knows how to make that catheter and its tubing very well. The company may make multiple kinds of catheters, using different kinds of tubing.

What happens if the company then decides to produce multilumen tubing for a new type of catheter? Level C is about figuring out how to make modifications to the process (in this case, using the same materials but a new extruding die), but on some level, those changes are still reactive. The company only managed the change because that's what's coming down the line, and such changes often bring with them problems to be resolved.

**Level B**. This is about proactively making changes. At level B, the company starts to employ Lean, Scrum, and Voice of Customer (VOC) concepts. People come up with ways to make the process better, cheaper, and more efficient. Leadership starts asking questions such as "Instead of the tube catheter taking two hours to build, how can it be done so efficiently that it only takes a half hour to build?"

Not only that, but now that the initial catheter can be built better, how can those processes be used to build the multilumen catheter better, more cheaply, and more efficiently? Then, how can those processes be used to make other items—and all with the same people on the production floor?

With each new level, the company also becomes more transparent. Everybody sees when changes are coming, allowing them to proactively make changes in their area.

**Level A.** This is when a company reaches the point where it uses metrics to predict change and, consequently, is benchmarked for its world-class processes. It's about proactively looking at the data generated by the processes, looking at what people are doing with Lean, and predicting next year's production very efficiently.

For example, perhaps you see an increase in nonconformance from a supplier whose parts you've used to build ten thousand items in a month. Your metrics may show that you're likely to have twenty complaints next year, causing you to lose 2 percent of sales. That information may help you decide to modify parts because the cost of rework is a savings over a single lost sale. Metrics help you see where processes need improving, where more training is needed, and where a shrinking workforce may dictate a need for new technology (and consequently more training).

## THE X-AXIS: COMPLIANCE WITH REQUIREMENTS

The X-axis is all about compliance with requirements. A medical device company may improve its processes but must meet all the requirements imposed on it by the different regulatory bodies in order to remain in the market.

The compliance with requirements levels are:

- **Level 1: Warning Letter**. The FDA sends warning letters for systemic noncompliance. These are for entire business processes that do not meet the regulatory requirements or when there is significant noncompliance in multiple processes. ISO audits find major nonconformance(s).

- **Level 2: 483/NC.** At the 483/NC level, the FDA issues 483 findings, but there are only areas of noncompliance (NC) and no systemic noncompliance. ISO audits find minor nonconformance(s).

- **Level 3: Compliant.** At the compliant level, your company meets all the major regulatory-required activities and processes, although minor corrections could still improve compliance.

- **Level 4: Bulletproof.** When your company is bulletproof, it meets all regulatory requirements and there is traceability from the requirements to their implementation.

- **Level 5: World Class.** A world-class company anticipates and leverages compliance requirements across multiple business systems. Processes are proactive, and your metrics give you action and alert triggers.

A company cannot be at level A on the Y-axis and still be at level 1 or 2 on the X-axis. A company reporting those results is experiencing what I call a state of "delusional improvement." That occurs when a company does not understand the requirements and it does not understand what is expected of it. It may document its requirements but has misinterpreted and/or does not meet the regulatory requirements in all the business systems and in all the geographies where they apply. Perhaps you've heard of companies suing the FDA? That's usually because they think the rules do not apply to them.

A company can, however, be at level 3 or 4 on the X-axis and be at level E or D on the Y-axis. However, when that happens, they experience what I call wasteful compliance. That is the attempt to inspect their way to quality by throwing a lot of resources into efforts to be compliant without ever making any real improvements. Wasteful compliance occurs when a company acquires another company and then develops a common Quality System to the lowest common denominator. The company pours resources into making business systems work in areas they were not designed for.

An example of wasteful compliance was a company that wanted to have a corporation-wide nonconformance process across its dozen manufacturing plants. Instead of using its common enterprise resource planning (ERP) system and building out a custom module, it bought a new software tool and hired a software company to design a process that was "bulletproof." The workflow had more than a dozen steps and more than sixty metadata fields, but only the Quality System personnel could access the tool. There was no integration with any other tools, and product lines and part numbers had to be manually added to the tool every month. Millions of dollars for what? A glorified spreadsheet. Eventually, compliance issues will arise in the company because the root cause was never addressed. There was no understanding of the requirements for the company's business processes.

## BREAK DOWN THE SILOS: ONE INFORMATION ARCHITECTURE FOR COMPANY-WIDE INTEGRATION

It's helpful to think of Consiliso as similar to having a single digital tablet with apps for performing different activities versus having dozens of separate tools that do not communicate with each other. Consiliso is the company framework for managing your information architecture, and in the tablet analogy, the apps are the business processes—some of those "apps" are core processes that are already included in Consiliso; others are electives based on the type of requirements that apply to your company.

By having one tool with all the information, you eliminate the need to validate all the separate tools, control roles and access in each tool, and there is no need to develop interfaces or move data between tools.

Figure 1-2 shows an analogy of how the information goes from separate paper systems to databases to a common platform (taking quality's continuous improvement from level E to level A, as in Figure 1-1). The common platform (the tablet) performs all the functions that each separate tool does. It may not be optimized for each, but the cost and interconnectivity outweigh minor decreased functionality. A common platform allows the addition of new information sources (i.e., apps) without the cost of a new tool, validation, and IT resources. The model shows how information silos break down into a common platform.

*Figure 1-2: Information Tools to Systems Analogy*

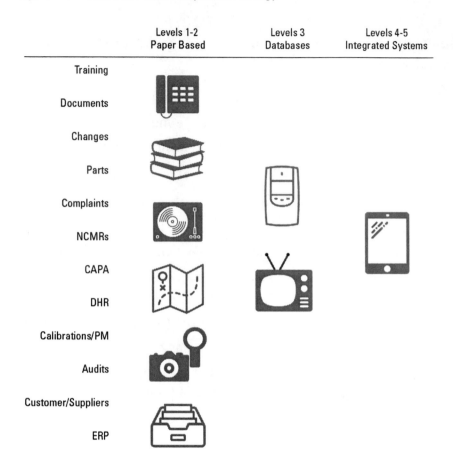

| | Levels 1-2<br>Paper Based | Levels 3<br>Databases | Levels 4-5<br>Integrated Systems |
|---|---|---|---|
| Training | | | |
| Documents | | | |
| Changes | | | |
| Parts | | | |
| Complaints | | | |
| NCMRs | | | |
| CAPA | | | |
| DHR | | | |
| Calibrations/PM | | | |
| Audits | | | |
| Customer/Suppliers | | | |
| ERP | | | |

Consiliso has defined all the possible business processes in a medical device company to help you design any kind of product, without reinventing processes or expanding into new markets.

For instance, a few years ago, Congress passed the Sunshine Act for reporting payments made to physicians by medical device companies for clinical trials, training, or other types of interaction. Many companies immediately felt they needed to build a separate process for the regulation. They believed they needed to hide that information from all but specific people within the company and publish reports separately and directly to the government and outside the public domain. Not true! Sunshine law reports are published in the public domain, so why would companies build a separate system to hide the information within the company? The belief that they needed a separate process was a reflex reaction to a new require-ment. Why duplicate your efforts and hide information that is published in the public domain? That just creates another level of bureaucracy and reduces trust within the company.

The sunshine laws are just another process, very easily inte-grated into Consiliso's business processes and master datasets. What do sunshine laws have to do with a Quality System? A great deal. Integrating them is a matter of using the same basic datasets of clinical trials, customers, products, and so on.

It may be difficult to determine what processes help a company operate efficiently and compliantly unless you have seen how integrated processes work. Solving the problem begins by understanding what business processes a company needs. But instead of creating a new process whenever a new problem or regulatory requirement comes along, with Consiliso you simply use and, when needed, modify the processes you already have.

## "OH NO, WE DO THAT"—HAS THIS HAPPENED TO YOU?

Most companies use a backroom for regulatory audits, which is essen-tially another conference room with a support person or team in charge of retrieving information requested by the auditors. That allows a point person or two to stay in the room with the auditors to answer questions.

Consiliso lets you do away with a backroom during an audit. Inspectors ask for many types of information very quickly. Instead of having "runners" retrieve paper files, set up a system in the audit room and assign someone the task of locating the record or object using a laptop to search your company's Quality System structures. By having the records easily retrievable, the auditor feels confident that the information is readily available for the whole company.

In one instance, a large medical device company using Consiliso completed an FDA Quality System Inspection Technique (QSIT) for a Class III product in twelve hours!

Is your company as transparent as it could be? Ask yourself these questions:

1. Does the mention of a new regulation make me want to close my office door and talk in whispers?

2. Does our Sunshine Act procedure involve publishing the information only internally? Or do we also publish it where it is accessible in the public domain?

3. Does everyone in your company know you have a five-year plan for your business: Sales, Quality System and Infrastructure?

4. How many people in our company could find and have immediate access to all the information needed for an FDA or ISO audit?

CHAPTER 2

# YOUR BUSINESS SYSTEMS: THEN AND NOW

A few years ago, I was working at a company in which every document was paper-based—all the product drawings, specifications, manufacturing work instructions, travelers, bill of materials (BOMs), device master records (DMRs), and change orders (COs). The documentation group consisted of three people who processed twelve product COs per month, with an average throughput of twenty-six days each to process the change from start to finish. The group also released about eighteen standard operating procedures (SOPs) and other reports each month. The engineers approved and released their own reports, which they compiled into design history file (DHF) binders stored in a fireproof cabinet. Needless to say, the documentation group's primary role was making and distributing photocopies.

One year after implementing Consiliso and expanding the product development efforts, all of the company's parts, documents, and COs were in a product lifecycle management (PLM) system. The same number of staff processed three hundred product and non-product COs per month, with an average throughput of four and a half days. Productivity of the documentation group increased by

1,000 percent, throughput decreased by more than 80 percent, and lost documents became a thing of the past.

Before Consiliso, the documentation group was so focused on accurate preparation of the documents that it could not see how it was creating a bottleneck in the process by delaying delivery of products to users. With the PLM tool in place, eliminating paper-based inefficiencies, the engineers and others were empowered to own their documents, leading to faster changes and, ultimately, to faster product development times. Engineers and others were able to do what they were paid to do: solve problems, rather than fight bureaucratic hurdles.

**The same number of staff processed three hundred product and non-product COs per month, with an average throughput of four and a half days.**

## THE EVOLUTION OF THE INDUSTRY

As have business systems, the medical device industry has also evolved. Medical devices have been around since the creation of the first surgical tools by the Greeks in the fifth century BCE. Starting in the 1800s with the advent of modern medical practices, companies began diversifying to meet modern needs. The modern medical device industry exploded in the 1960s. Some technologies back then were actually spinoffs from the US space program. Companies that developed devices such as the implantable pacemaker, external defibrillator, balloon catheter, and CT scanner found a huge untapped market in using technology to make people's lives better.

In 1961, the FDA gained the authority to regulate medical device clinical trials and related methodologies. Prior to that, no premarket approval or product review processes existed. Some fifteen years later, in 1976, in response to a rash of product field issues, the FDA introduced the medical device Good Manufacturing Practices (GMP) requirements, which regulated product quality for all medical devices. The FDA also published Good Laboratory Practices (GLP) and Good Clinical Practices (GCP) regulations, known collectively as GXP, which regulated formal documentation of manufacturers' businesses, processes, and builds.

At the time, documenting procedures involved typewriters and handwritten approvals; any word processing ran only on a mainframe computer. Business procedure documents were, typically, topped by a cover page listing revision history, effective date, and approvers, and the change information was buried somewhere within the documentation.

Paper documents were owned and stored by each department, usually in boxes and file cabinets. Design drawings, specifications, and manufacturing instructions were managed by different groups and connected only by a paper CO. The CO process involved many people, including a person assigning numbers, copy-room personnel, drafters, checkers, and CO administrators.

Most companies documented their records in some sort of logbook—paper, of course. The logbook records were written in pencil to enable revision number changes without the need to replace an entire page.

My first medical device organization position in the late 1980s was at a company where one person had the task of managing the company's eight-inch-thick document logbook. She ensured that all revisions and change dates were recorded, and she was consulted any time a document's change history was needed. She was, essentially, the company's document search engine.

With the introduction of the personal computer in the 1980s, database applications converted paper logs into electronic information. Those initial tools, while useful, were still isolated and, ultimately, only aided paper-based processes. They did not have workflow, hyperlinks, or electronic signature capabilities.

As people grew more comfortable with technology, a business process reengineering craze hit all industries. However, simply reengineering a business process did not necessarily discover or fix the underlying problems. Reengineering a process may only make an inefficient paper system electronic. Or it may make a process "easier" to use by putting it on the company's intranet or "in the cloud." Applying Lean concepts to a process may reduce the number of existing steps.

All these efforts help improve a process, but in order to make a reengineering effort effective, all the requirements must be identified across all the possible regulations, and the business processes must be architected to maximize reuse across the company. That is the essence of Consiliso.

## REGULATIONS TODAY

Many types of regulation apply to businesses in today's world. These include regulations on labor, tax, health, and safety. Medical device companies and state-of-the-art manufacturing companies also follow Quality System standards and regulations. These standards and regulations require companies to have defined business and manufacturing processes that are documented using procedures, forms, and controlled records.

While Quality System standards and regulations cover processes related to devices, other business regulations have the same basic rules.

For instance, when implementing a Sarbanes-Oxley (SOX) compliance procedure, a safety form, or clinical trial record, you must manage and store the information in much the same way as you do your device Quality System records. The best companies also use these same basic processes for human resources, information systems, and legal processes.

## CONFIGURATION MANAGEMENT

The concept of controlling and reusing master information across product design and manufacturing is the basis of what is known as configuration management.

Configuration management started in the US military in the 1950s as a way to build complex airplanes and rockets that worked every time. That type of manufacturing requires an extreme level of detail because field repairs are often not an option, and errors could have deadly results for a pilot or equipment operator.

As it applies to business leadership, configuration management is a way for company executives to make sense of their business knowledge because different areas organize the same information, according to their own methods and requirements.

Case in point: In the 1990s, a pacemaker company I worked for purchased another pacemaker company. The acquiring company planned to take the technology from the acquired company and then shut that operation down. The documents and information in the company I worked for were mostly electronic and organized in a specific way. I traveled to the acquired company to inventory its documentation and bring it into our system. For two days, I walked around the operations there and finally came up with a list of some fifty different storage locations for the documents we needed. They included various standalone computers and network drives in various departments. Biocompatibility test reports, I found, were kept in a file drawer and organized as a handwritten list in a laboratory logbook. Much of the information was the same as that used in my company, but it was organized in a completely different way. That's what commonly happens when companies or divisions merge.

The beauty of Consiliso is that it works for companies of any size. Small companies, normally, use only the basic parts of the system, but larger companies employ more processes as needs demand. When companies join, Consiliso helps make sense of the information and brings business systems together. So if, for instance, a Class II medical device company acquires a Class III medical device maker, the Class II maker simply expands its Quality System to encompass the new Class III requirements without having to build an entirely new system from scratch.

Admittedly, reconfiguring a company's systems is a little like opening up your hall closet and finding it in complete disarray. But with Consiliso, the fix is relatively easy. It involves, essentially, doing a closet purge. That means pulling everything out of the closet, taking an inventory of it all, and then reorganizing how everything goes back in. Some items may need new cubbies or shelves, you might add a second hanging rod, and some things you will toss. And, while we're at it, we'll make space for items we know we will need in the future: kids' hockey sticks and skates, for instance. For those, we just add racks off to the side. We don't have to rebuild the closet itself; all we have to do is rework how things are organized on the inside and reconfigure some of the space for current and future needs.

## THE TROUBLE WITH QUALITY MANAGEMENT SYSTEMS

In the mid-1970s, compliance for medical device makers primarily focused on manufacturing. But when recall issues repeatedly pointed to flaws in design rather than in the manufacturing process, the regulations changed in the mid-1990s to look at design *and* manufacturing. Today, the regulations are more quality-focused, not just compliance-focused.

The first international standard to describe a Quality Management System was ISO 9000, based on the British standard BS 5750 and released in 1987. In 1990, the US Congress passed the Safe Medical Device Act, which led to the introduction of the Quality System Regulation (QSR) 21CFR 820, which became effective in 1997. A series of regulations applicable to the whole medical device product life cycle followed—from planning to design to manufacturing to obsolescence. The FDA definition of a Quality System is "the organizational structure, responsibilities, procedures, processes, and resources for implementing quality management."[1]

But Consiliso is more than a Quality System. In the old days, companies had a fifty-page quality manual and one hundred to one thousand procedures. With Consiliso, there is one small quality manual and fifteen to twenty business process documents. The procedures integrate with those processes. That's Consiliso.

---

1    21CFR820.3 (v), CFR - Code of Federal Regulations, U.S. Food & Drug Administration Title 21, vol. 8 (April 1, 2016), accessed May 3, 2017, https://www.accessdata.fda.gov/scripts/cdrh/cfdocs/cfCFR/CFRSearch.cfm?fr=820.3.

Regulatory requirements are *multiplying* as more countries adopt Quality System regulations for products sold in their country, which is impacting medical device manufacturers and other regulated manufacturers. The explosion in similar but different regulations and standards results in the proliferation of company policies and procedures and creates more complex business processes. That results in the creation of policies and procedures that are directly tied to the implementation of each *separate* business system and applicable regulations.

**With Consiliso, there is one small quality manual and fifteen to twenty business process documents. The procedures integrate with those processes. That's Consiliso.**

Here is an analogy of what happens to your Quality Systems over time. You started building a house with the original Good Manufacturing Practices (GMPs). You built a nice kitchen and living room. But then the Medical Devices Directive (MDD) came along and required you to have three bedrooms and a bath. Then the FDA changed the GMP to the QSR, and now you have to add a basement and a bathroom off the kitchen. Then, with ISO 13485, you need a laundry room and a garage. Now add the requirements and procedures for environmental, safety, and financial controls.

What does the final house look like?

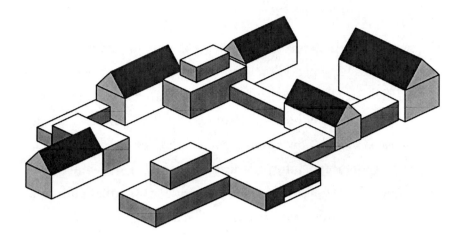

What began with a set of specs for a conventional house changed over time until the end result was a hodgepodge of randomly stacked, incongruent structures laid out in an inefficient, difficult-to-navigate configuration.

The house does everything required, except it does not flow, it is difficult to maintain, and it is hard to change. There are redundancies and bottlenecks. It would take a team of people to guide an inspector through the structure and its systems. And forget about curb appeal!

Only so much business process reengineering can be done successfully when different groups within a company interpret new requirements, procedures are owned and changed by various groups, and standards keep evolving. (Note: ISO 9001 updates every ten years.) There are hundreds of examples of companies spending millions of dollars implementing the latest tool, only to have it rejected by users.

## TRIBAL KNOWLEDGE

The problem with companies experiencing disconnectedness is that they are stuck in what John Dew discussed in his article "Tribal Quest." He described "tribal cultures" as operating as closed systems. A closed system, he wrote, is determined by "how information and knowledge is shared, how power is gained and held, and how formal rules are ignored and informal rules are enforced to maintain the status quo." [2] Dew also described hallmarks of a tribal culture as "local control of information and sequestering of knowledge . . . . While procedures may exist as something to show auditors, they're not really used . . . . The experienced employees in the tribal culture maintain their own notes about how processes work and how to get things done in the company. Employees mark settings on equipment with pencils and use sticky notes to communicate between shifts."[3]

According to Dew, individuals in a tribal culture are encouraged to work around problems while ignoring the cause—forget about correcting it. What's worse is that they are actually rewarded for overlooking problems.[4] "Within the tribal organization," he wrote, "it's normal to suppress information about the existence and nature of problems."[5]

## LEARNING TO TRUST AMID THE CHAOS

What happens within any company is best described as chaos. Plans are developed and implemented, but what actually happens and when is unknown. External stakeholders often exert influence that

---

2    Dew, John, "Tribal Quest," *Quality Progress,* 2011.

3    Ibid.

4    Ibid.

5    Ibid.

changes a company's plans in small or large ways. Employees leave the company, new people come in, contractors and consultants are hired—each of these changes and modifies how the plan is implemented.

**What happens within any company is best described as chaos.**

But chaos also helps manage companies, as explained by Meg Wheatley in *Leadership and the New Science*: "If organizations are machines, control makes sense. If organizations are process structures, then seeking to impose control through permanent structure is suicide. If we believe that acting responsibly means exerting control by having our hands into everything, then we cannot hope for anything except what we already have—a treadmill of effort and life-destroying stress."[6]

Chaos in an organization does not mean people do whatever they want. It means strange attractors (placed boundaries) control where the process goes, even though where it is at any point in time is not always predictable. Efficient and compliant processes are achieved by 1) defining processes with correct requirements, and 2) establishing policies with the right kind of metrics. That kind of process design does not give you consistent results every day, but it does produce an *overall* improving and controlled process.

The company grows when leadership willingly gives up micro-managing activities and allows people to use the inherent flexibility in a well-designed process. As Wheatley explains, "New understandings of change and disorder are also emerging from chaos theory. Work in this field, which keeps expanding to take in more areas of inquiry,

---

6    Wheatley, Margaret, *Leadership and the New Science: Discovering Order in a Chaotic World* (San Francisco: Berrett-Koehler, 1992), 11.

has led to a new appreciation of the relationship between order and chaos. These two forces are now understood as mirror images, one containing the other, a continual process where a system can leap into chaos and unpredictability yet, within that state, be held within parameters that are well ordered and predictable."[7]

One of the large companies I worked for had a hard-and-fast process for controlling nonconforming material: Only certain people actually entered and transacted a nonconformance. That led to a lack of reporting because people might discover a nonconformance but then forget to notify one of the few people approved to enter and transact it. Or, they might discover something that did not meet requirements and yet was not defined as nonconformance, so it was not reported. For example, a part was the right size but the wrong color, and color was not defined as a nonconformance. The system was so controlled that things got lost and bad product made it out the door. In other words, too much constraint without allowing for variables led to a loss of control.

The opposite happened at another company. There, I set up the system so that anyone in the company could create a nonconformance in about thirty seconds. All it took was a few clicks. If people thought it was a bad idea to use a part, they were able to start the process for involving Quality and move on to their next task. Customer complaints related to nonconforming materials decreased.

Chaos theory is about a business having the ability to constantly adapt to changing technology, requirements, and other unknowns. Systems must have the ability to evolve with the changing business environment.

---

7    Wheatley, Margaret, *Leadership and the New Science: Discovering Order in a Chaotic World* (San Francisco: Berrett-Koehler, 1992), 11.

Sometimes, you don't know what you don't know when you build a process. But Consiliso is flexible; it allows you to expand the process so you don't have to start everything from scratch again.

Admittedly, working with chaos requires a level of trust in the organization. Does company management trust the employees? Do employees trust management? Do departments that feed each other information or materials trust each other? Trust in an organization is the foundation for implementing change. And the faster you implement change, the faster you grow.

## ESTABLISHING TRUST: BREAK DOWN THE SILOS

One way to institute trust within your business processes is to remove the information silos, which I discussed in Chapter 1, "Consiliso: What It Is, What It Means to You." Information silos are those areas of the company in which only the person controlling the information has the power to disseminate it. That occurs whether the information is paper-based or digital. Digital information is controlled when users are assigned specific roles that allow limited access to all or part of a database. Defined users and roles, limited software licenses, and restricted access to information in your company create silos that, ultimately, stifle your company's forward progression.

In order to break down these silos, *everyone* needs access to *all the information they need* to do their job.

Back in the 1990s, I was an engineer working to resolve a product issue. I needed to copy a major chunk of information from the product user manual into my report. I went to the marketing group that controlled writing the manual to get an electronic copy. I was told I could not have a copy because 1) the PDF version of the file in their vault was not the official version—even though the documentation group referenced the file, it did not have a copy; and 2) the official version was in Adobe Illustrator, which I did not have on my computer. The fastest way for me to obtain the information I needed was to request a paper manual from inventory and then retype the section out of the manual to add to my investigation results. That's the kind of damage a silo inflicts.

That experience led me to make it my mission to develop a Quality System where most documentation is made available to everyone in the company. Only the most sensitive remains "under lock and key." That's Consiliso.

Consiliso is an *open system* where everyone has a license and is allowed to view everything they need. Only certain types of information are locked down. A *closed system* is one that makes users ask permission to see any information their "tribe" does not own. Having one tool with all the information eliminates the need to validate all the separate tools, control roles and access in each tool, and to develop interfaces to move data between tools.

Silos are often little more than power plays to force people to seek out one person for information. An engineer who worked at a medical device company that did not have Consiliso recently shared with me an example of multiple silos that created real hurdles. The engineer was given a week to resolve a field issue, and in that time, she had to obtain information from four different sources: a regulatory group, the complaint group, and two different document control groups. Two weeks later, she still did not have all the information she needed despite filling out the proper forms to obtain copies of files or have IT grant her access to various software tools in which the information resided.

Conversely, using Consiliso in a similar situation, I was able to bring up everything I needed in a few minutes to answer questions while talking to a doctor on the phone about an issue. All the files, the device history record (DHR), photos, and test results were available to me with just a few clicks of a mouse. Even though I was an executive with access to information restricted to high-level employees, none of the information I needed for that phone call was in the restricted part of the system. Anyone in the Engineering, Quality, Regulatory, or Clinical departments would have been able to look at any and all of those documents.

## MORE IS NOT BETTER

As I mentioned before, implementing Consiliso begins with an assessment of the company's processes. That involves spending a couple of weeks figuring out how the company works and then mapping everything out to show the relationships between the processes.

Companies may opt to do their own assessment internally. Or, they may hire the assessment out to a third party—for example, CMMI Institute, an organization working on a maturity model assessment for the medical device industry.

The assessment involves an inventory, of sorts, of a company's operations to determine how the work is done and what that work generates in terms of information. Where is the data? Who has access to it? Those are some of the questions asked to help determine where the holes are and design the system to fix those holes.

The goal in using Consiliso is to plan better up front and avoid delusional improvement and wasteful compliance. It's about more than just being compliant; it is about being more efficient, saving costs, and making the company more scalable. In short, it's about making everyone's life easier. In the end, that makes the company more compliant because it solves problems better and faster for patients and doctors. Let me share with you a couple of stories now about how delusional improvement and wasteful compliance affected companies with closed systems.

In a case of delusional improvement, a company spent more than $2 million to design and implement an interface between its enterprise resource planning (ERP) system and the labeling system for the production floor in order to solve labeling errors. The system was supposed to print out the correct label when the product entered that work center step. Unfortunately, there were so many options in processing the work order that the interface always had errors. Nonconformance for labeling, rework, and label-related customer complaints abounded. Using Consiliso at another company, we fixed a very similar problem with complex serialized labeling by adding a job information barcode on the paper job traveler. The operator on the floor scanned the barcode at the labeling work center and printed the correct label every time. Instead of the company trying to do everything electronically, it made the paper job traveler the data interface tool!

As for wasteful compliance, at one company where I worked, many errors began appearing on COs. So, the Quality Director, in a knee-jerk reaction, required that all approver's managers also sign each one. Not only did that double approvers from seven to fourteen, slowing the process, but it did not improve quality. At one point, I was required to sign a CO for a procedure outside my area of responsibility. Twelve people had already approved the change, but I decided to check with the engineer who knew the topic because he was not on the list of approvers. Sure enough, he found an error. Talk about wasteful compliance! That was a case of "more is not better." Designing a good process, having transparency, and assigning responsibilities appropriately leads to better, faster, and more efficient results.

## REBUILD YOUR COMPANY'S QUALITY SYSTEM: CONSILISO IS YOUR ARCHITECT

Instead of the hodgepodge house I described earlier, Consiliso concepts allow you to build an efficiently run "office building" for your company. Consiliso is your architect. It contains the blueprints tailored to your company's needs, and it makes it easy to upgrade your systems when your company scales.

Consiliso concepts help you build your company's Quality Systems by

- □ breaking down preconceived notions on how to implement the requirements of applicable laws, regulations, guidance, standards, and internal policies.

- □ providing a complete set of blueprints for every aspect (what, why, and how) of work within your company.

- □ making information transparent company-wide while providing the ability to quickly adopt changes.

- □ achieving modular and reusable business processes and master datasets across all business functions.

- □ moving management controls to key business process metrics, instead of only financial considerations.

Equate Consiliso with the construction of an office building: Start by choosing a location. Location represents your industry and products. When you select a location, you define the regulations and standards you need to follow.

Once you define your location, you design the building and determine how all the building systems work. Each of your defined business systems (quality, environmental, financial, etc.) are floors in the building.

Every building requires standardized systems for the electrical, plumbing, HVAC, lighting, data network, security, fire suppression, elevators, and façade design. You must meet building codes and standards to implement these "utilities."

The control center in the basement manages the building. The control center receives data from all of the building systems either electronically or by people in the control center who "audit" the building.

The control center is the concept of management processes: It adjusts and modifies the utilities across the floors to provide the most productive work environment.

## OTHER BUILDING UTILITIES IN
## BUSINESS PROCESSES

- HVAC = Documentation. The correct temperature controls allow people to do their job efficiently.

- Data Network = Records Management. Data stores what you did.

- Lighting = Training. Light enables people to see what they need to do.

- Security = Audit Processes. Guards provide feedback on how well the systems and processes work.

- Wall/Floor Structure = Standards/Requirements Management. The physical features control what can and cannot be done.

- Electricity = Financial Accounting. Electricity is the money that makes the company run.

- Elevator and Stairs = HR Management Processes. The physical movement of people represents the jobs that people do in the different business systems.

- Plumbing/Bathrooms = Issue Management and CAPA Processes. People need a way to deal with things that do not normally occur in their process.

Product development, manufacturing, and other product-related processes that directly support the customers' needs represent the *real work* done in the building. The building utilities (support processes) affect all of these product-related processes.

There are multiple components to a company's business systems. The next three chapters are going to focus on just three of these, three floors of the office building, if you will: product quality, clinical trials, and finance.

## "OH NO, WE DO THAT"—HAS THIS HAPPENED TO YOU?

Medical device companies are expected to engage in Quality System management reviews—meetings that, basically, review the company's quality metrics and look for systemic problems. Unfortunately, especially in very large companies, the meetings are eight hours long and involve a review of every product line. Even then, managers often leave the meeting with no real information or action items.

With Consiliso, the same review takes a fraction of the time and is easily displayed on a color-coded dashboard that serves as a great visual for areas that are on track or that need improvement. The dashboard allows the executive team to understand the scope and complexity of improvements needed in order to achieve compliance (and eventually, Consiliso). The dashboard is used over the entire implementation of *any* business system.

Do you come away from your Quality System management reviews with action items for improving your processes? Always ask yourself these questions:

1. Do we cover all our metrics?

2. What is our compliance rate?

3. How long does our management review take? (This includes the length of time required to assemble all the information the review meeting requires.)

4.    Who attends our management reviews?

5.    Do our metrics actually show our trends?

CHAPTER 3

# THE PRODUCT QUALITY SYSTEM

Back in the 1990s, I was a documentation manager working with product development teams. My group was made up of drafters, technical writers, and configuration management specialists. The role of the configuration management specialist was to help every product development team ensure all the parts and documents needed for the project were defined, numbered, and structured in a DMR and DHF hierarchy. The structuring allowed everyone to understand the impact of changes on the product design.

The database application we used back then gave us "where used" information and BOM structures, but they were shown in separate, tabular formats. The entire product hierarchy was not shown in a graphical format, which would have allowed all the components and interactions to be seen at once.

To have that graphic representation readily available, the configuration specialists took it upon themselves to create an organizational chart, or blueprint, of the product structure on an 11" x 17" sheet of paper. The blueprint included document, part, and assembly numbers, along with pictures of the subassemblies. The specialists made copies of the blueprint and posted them inside every product development team member's cubicle. That helped everyone find information quickly and understand the relationship between a product's parts and documents. Ultimately, that helped improve overall compliance to the product development process. Still, it was static, so in the end, it wasn't as efficient as having a flexible, digital system to provide up-to-date answers with a few clicks.

## BLUEPRINTS FOR A COMPLEX STRUCTURE

That 11" x 17" sheet of paper comprised what was, essentially, the product DMR. Similarly, your Quality System is seen in "blueprints" that show your company's business process hierarchy, information process flow, and assessment status.

**Can you imagine *not* having blueprints and 3-D models to describe a complex structure before it is built?**

Can you imagine *not* having blueprints and 3-D models to describe a complex structure before it is built? Think about designing a new building: Isn't it much easier to build the structure to work effectively when you start with blueprints and 3-D models that give you a big-picture view of the structure and its components and then let you drill down to see how everything works? Wouldn't your life be easier with a digital blueprint of your Quality System, a high-level view of all the business processes in your company that also provides the ability to drill down to the details?

**Unfortunately, in most companies, the Quality System is composed of a paper manual some fifty pages long.**

Unfortunately, in most companies, the Quality System is composed of a paper manual some fifty pages long. Digging into the details about a process is a matter of perusing a table of contents and then flipping through pages and pages, and then finding another referenced document to get an answer. It's a tedious process. Even worse, for some companies, the Quality System "manual" is just a list of documents, and the only way to get the details about a process is to figure out (usually by guessing) which document applies. With either of these manual methods, it's difficult to find what you need to know about a process without a clear understanding of all the connections involved. That is why companies develop "shadow" Quality Systems—it is too hard to follow the documented processes.

When someone needs to get from point A to point B in your company, a paper diagram with a list of steps will eventually get them there. But most people really need a blueprint to digitally take them by the hand and get them where they need to go to get the job done. That's what Consiliso does.

It's crucial to understand how the business processes work and how information flows in a company. Your business process owners need to understand how their business processes affect others in the company. They need to know where their inputs come from and where their outputs go. Figure 3-1 provides a high-level "blueprint" showing the complexity of your company's Quality System.

Figure 3-1: Quality System Process Interaction Blueprint

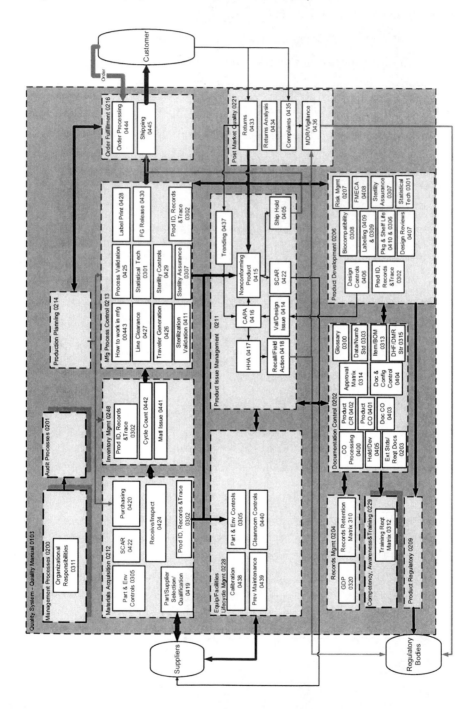

The concepts of Consiliso are based on electrical engineering's system engineering concept. The idea is to break complex systems into manageable chunks and show the relationships between the chunks.

Similarly, Product Quality Systems appear extremely complicated from a high-level view. But closer inspection reveals that the smaller boxes inside the diagram (Figure 3-1) represent the inner workings of a medical device company. Those smaller boxes represent the processes in the company—management processes, audit processes, production planning, and more—and show how they connect to each other. The various procedures associated with each process are within the processes (identified by document number). Those processes and procedures appear in the Consiliso Quality System Assessment Matrix (Figure 3-2). This dashboard helps you better understand the overall health of your company. Instead of just looking at issues such as compliance and quality, the matrix looks at your business process robustness and maturity.

## Figure 3-2: Sample Quality System Assessment Matrix

| TYPES | BUSINESS PROCESSES | REQTS DEFINED | GOALS DEFINED | GOALS MET |
|---|---|---|---|---|
| Process | Management Processes | | | |
| Process | Audit Processes | | | |
| Process | Document Control Policies | | | |
| Procedure | Quality System Documents | | | |
| Procedure | Merch Design Print | | | |
| Procedure | Software Design Print | | | |
| Procedure | MP/IPs | | | |
| Procedure | Mfg Reqts | | | |
| Procedure | Test Reqts | | | |
| Procedure | Design Reports | | | |
| Procedure | Hold/Deviation | | | |
| Procedure | Change Planning | | | |
| Procedure | Change Implementation | | | |
| Process | Records Mgmt Processes | | | |
| Process | Scientific and Product Research | | | |
| Process | Product Development Processes | | | |
| Procedure | Design Controls | | | |
| Procedure | Design Reviews | | | |
| Procedure | Risk Management | | | |
| Procedure | Labeling Creation | | | |
| Procedure | Packaging | | | |
| Procedure | Sterilization Validation | | | |
| Procedure | Biocompatibility | | | |
| Procedure | Engineering Reports/V&V | | | |
| Procedure | Design Issue Mgmt | | | |
| Procedure | DHF Controls | | | |
| Process | Product Release Process | | | |
| Process | Product Issue Mgmt Processes | | | |
| Procedure | NCMR | | | |
| Procedure | CAPA | | | |
| Procedure | HHA | | | |
| Procedure | Recall/Field Action | | | |
| Process | Materials Acquisition and Control | | | |
| Procedure | Supplier Assurance/AVL | | | |
| Procedure | Purchasing | | | |
| Procedure | Incoming DHR/Lot Labeling | | | |
| Procedure | SCAR | | | |
| Process | Inventory Management Processes | | | |
| Procedure | Lot Labeling | | | |
| Process | Manufacturing Process Control Processes | | | |
| Procedure | Process Development/PFMECA | | | |
| Procedure | Process Validation | | | |
| Procedure | Traveler Generation | | | |
| Procedure | Line Clearance/Document Access | | | |
| Procedure | Label Printing | | | |
| Procedure | Sterilization Controls (BI, LAL, Bioburden) | | | |
| Procedure | FG release | | | |
| Procedure | Trending/SPC | | | |
| Process | Order Fulfillment Processes | | | |
| Process | Import and Export Processes | | | |
| Process | Post Market Quality Processes | | | |

*This table is for illustrative purposes only.*

The rows in the matrix list business processes and key procedures and sub-procedures. The columns list the attributes and maturity of the processes and procedures.

The matrix lets you view your company as a system, not just processes and procedures that need improving. Use color coding to provide a quick view of how well your system is working, with red indicating a systemic issue, yellow a compliance issue, and green acceptable performance.

When implementing the matrix, many companies start off "seeing red," an indication of areas in need of review. The goal, of course, is to turn the cells from red to yellow to green. Within a year or two of redefining business processes and updating tools, most companies achieve a matrix that is more than 50 percent green. One company using Consiliso saw its matrix reach a level of 90 percent green over a five-year span.

The more green the matrix displays, the more your company moves to the upper right corner of the Maturity and Compliance Matrix that I diagrammed in Figure 1-1, in Chapter 1, "Consiliso: What It Is, What It Means to You."

## THE KEY TO COMPLIANCE AND CONTINUOUS IMPROVEMENT

When it comes to operating a company on a day-to-day basis, some companies prefer to push the envelope. They make a conscious decision not to go the extra mile and employ best practices for their operations. For instance, one executive told me, "Hey, 483s are good; they tell you what you need to fix."

But an effective and efficient Quality System is the key to compliance and continuous improvement.

More than one million companies are certified to the ISO 9001 and ISO 13485 Quality System standards. In medical device companies, the ISO 13485 Quality System standard, along with the FDA Quality System Regulations (QSR), drive the requirements of a common set of business processes. The FDA tracks over twenty-five thousand medical device companies in its Establishment Registration and Device Listing database.[8]

The ISO 9001 Quality Management System requirements are broader than ISO 13485, because 13485 was tailored for the medical device industry from ISO 9001. Consiliso uses ISO 9001 to provide oversight for the ISO 13485 Product Quality System. For the most part, ISO 13485 is harmonized with ISO 9001, but there are differences. The major difference is that ISO 9001 requires a company to demonstrate continual improvement and has requirements for customer satisfaction, while ISO 13485 does not. Both ISO standards require definition of your business process interactions and that those processes be suitable, adequate, and effective in meeting the requirements of the standards.

With medical device companies operating in the United States, the FDA has a say in your Product Quality System. Today, the ISO

---

8    "Establishment Registration & Device Listing," U.S. Food & Drug Administration, accessed June 20, 2017, https://www.accessdata.fda.gov/scripts/cdrh/cfdocs/cfRL/TextSearch.cfm.

13485 and the FDA regulations for medical device companies are almost identical.

There are many definitions and requirements for a medical device Quality System from the directives and regulatory bodies. I won't go into depth on them in this book, but they are spelled out in great detail in the Consiliso textbook, found at Consiliso.com.

While the ISO standards define a Quality System as the organizational structure, procedures, processes, and resources needed to implement quality management, these international standards for quality management require you to use the "process approach." For a company to function effectively, it must identify, execute, and manage numerous processes. In fact, the output from one process often forms the input for the next process. The process approach involves the application of the system of processes within a company, together with the identification of interactions and the management of those processes.

Unified, well-designed, and integrated processes are the essence of Consiliso. The Consiliso Quality System is the blueprint for meeting the ISO 9001, ISO 13485, and FDA QSR Quality System standards.

Consider the building analogy from the last chapter: When you construct the building for your company, you must meet certain city building codes. The codes, for instance, specify parameters for the water-supply lines, drain lines, electricity, and other utilities that equip the

> The Consiliso Quality System is the blueprint for meeting the ISO 9001, ISO 13485, and FDA QSR Quality System standards.

building. In understanding how the building is constructed, would you rather try to read and decipher a list of building codes? Or, would you rather review the blueprints to see the design of the building? The documents in your current Product Quality System tell you how to build and operate a building; Consiliso gives you the blueprints for the building. And the blueprints are the *right* blueprints for medical device companies.

A Product Quality System based on the ISO and FDA regulations is fairly complex and must provide management, oversight, and planning to help you design, build, and service products. An effective Quality System helps eliminate redundancies and reduces corrective actions. That's something I've seen in numerous medical device manufacturing facilities.

For instance, when analyzing the corrective and preventive action (CAPA) process in one large company, I found six separate CAPA processes. There were CAPA processes for suppliers, on-site manufacturing, off-site manufacturing, complaints/returns, design, and continuation engineering. Without a common process or tool providing formal documentation or shared investigation results, people working in the company had no visibility into what was happening outside their own area. One problem that arose in the company was actually "solved" three times by three different teams over a ten-year period. None of the teams knew what the other teams had done! Unfortunately, the multiple CAPA processes eventually led to a warning letter for the company because a problem "solved" in the supplier CAPA affected manufacturing and resulted in subsequent field complaints.

Your Product Quality System needs to resolve complex issues across products, functions, and technologies. But cumbersome business processes actually slow down problem resolution. Bringing humor to the situation, a former associate of mine, Dale Hougham, formulated what he called his "five steps of a dysfunctional corrective action system."

1. **Denial**. Deny the problem exists.

2. **Refute the data**. Question the data or how it was collected.

3. **Blame the customer**. Assume the product was misused.

4. **Haggle over the corrective action plan**. Debate the fix among all groups.

5. **Miss the window of opportunity**. Challenge the payback, given the delays in implementation and, ultimately, convince yourself it's too late to do anything!

Do these five steps sound a little too familiar? Have you seen them in action? They may seem absurd in an ethical medical device company, but I have seen these occur many times at many different companies over my career.

A benefit of using Consiliso is that you start with a blueprint for all possible processes and then tailor the Quality System to suit your company's needs.

For instance, if your company decides to make a combination medical device with a drug (a.k.a, a combo device), then your Quality System needs additional processes to accommodate the pharmaceuticals regulations that control drug manufacturing. Those processes may include Current Good Manufacturing Practices (cGMP), which are special regulations of the FDA and other countries outside the United States.

I know of a medical device contract manufacturer that only made standard medical devices but wanted to get into combo devices; it set up its Quality System as a one-size-fits-all. The company decided that one Quality System that incorporated the device and drug requirements in *all* of its processes (even for products without a drug component) would be easier to use. That led to major changes in everything from the tools used in manufacturing to the business processes. The costs to run the combo device Quality System were higher than a standard medical device Quality System. The company began losing business in the standard medical devices market because of its burdensome requirements. That one-size-fits-all methodology ended up costing the company 75 percent of its medical device business.

The moral of that story? Understand the requirements needed for the products you make—that's what goes into your Quality System. If all the business is not involved in the manufacturing of combo devices, then only specific business processes of the Quality System need to change.

Understanding the Quality System requirements is crucial when they vary slightly based on other industries. For instance, the Federal Aviation Administration's (FAA) Quality System does not align with medical device Quality Systems. That's important to know for makers of automated external defibrillators (AEDs) because airplanes are required to carry them. At one point, I needed

**That one-size-fits-all methodology ended up costing the company 75 percent of its medical device business.**

to resolve the problem of dealing with two different Quality Systems for one company, so I created an *FAA Product Quality Manual* to accommodate the separate requirements instead of altering the existing Quality System to FAA regulations.

Consiliso makes it easy to manage the concept of separate Quality Systems, which I also refer to as business systems, because the business processes are scalable. The FDA and ISO 13485 business systems are also known as the Product Quality System. Consiliso allows you to architect and design your Product Quality System to be whatever your company needs to meet ISO, FDA, and applicable international requirements, and to efficiently solve problems while avoiding wasteful compliance and delusional improvement. Consiliso expands the concept of business systems into other areas because, for instance, you may need an environmental business system to meet ISO 14000 requirements or a financial business system to meet SOX requirements. Consiliso defines fourteen business systems that are applicable to medical device companies. However, only the largest companies use that many business systems. Most companies just use a few.

Your Product Quality System ultimately reflects your image to your customers and regulators—your company's "curb appeal." It helps people know exactly what to expect from your company in the way of quality, consistency, efficiency, and value. With well-designed processes, people know what to expect when they interact with your company in terms of customer service, quality of product, quality of shipment, labeling, and returns. Your Product Quality System is designed to help you sell

**Consiliso defines the correct level of granularity of content, policy, metrics, and mapping to effectively manage your processes and help keep your doors open.**

medical devices that adhere to regulations and give your company value in the market.

That's the basic role of a Product Quality System for a medical device manufacturer: to ensure the consistent provision of safe products to patients. Consiliso defines the correct level of granularity of content, policy, metrics, and mapping to effectively manage your processes and help keep your doors open.

## AVOID SHADOW QUALITY SYSTEMS

Are the procedures and business systems in your company aligned, or do they make your people do twice the amount of work needed? Do your Product Quality System procedures require your people to do a task one way, just to get it done, but then document it differently for the sake of the auditors? If so, then you're operating with a shadow Quality System, and you're on your way to having a product fail.

Shadow Quality Systems exist when, for instance, a procedure is written in a way that leaves out information. For example, a form that is supposed to be filled out on the manufacturing floor has ambiguous instructions or leaves out space to report on a key metric that the employees have been instructed to monitor. Someone in manufacturing may know there's a problem with a product on the supply side of operations, but without the procedure for reporting the issue, they simply complete their area of responsibility and then move the product on. Some companies are so worried about how they control operations that they are guilty of straight-jacketing people—CAPAs become legal documents governing operations instead of viable tools to solve problems because the company is only worried about what is on the FDA's radar or what is discoverable in a lawsuit.

Shadow Quality Systems are eliminated with Consiliso because it lets you map out your company's business processes, providing visibility and transparency across the business systems. That also allows your company's maturity level to improve over time.

## METRICS MOVE YOU TO HIGHER MATURITY

Every one of your business processes needs a metric, or KPI. Those metrics must have goals to show that the process is adequate, suitable, and effective. How those metrics are reported and measured moves the company into higher maturity levels and a more proactive culture. But metrics actually come in three forms: good, bad, and ugly.

Good metrics drive a company to improve its processes. Bad metrics just state the status of the company and do not drive improvements. Ugly metrics seem appropriate on the surface, but instead, drive behavior in the wrong direction. An example of an ugly metric is "reduce the throughput time for COs." On the surface, this seems like a good metric to make the COs flow better and get changes implemented faster. The problem is that the CO process is an implementation step in the overall product development or issue management processes. Examples of good metrics include "reduce the number of post-product release changes for new products" or "reduce the time from product issues identification to product change implementation." Creating a metric in the middle of the process without understanding the ramifications for the whole process drives poor decision-making. Consiliso provides the visibility for you to see the connections between the processes, helping you better understand the impact one makes on another.

A classic example of good, bad, and ugly metrics is in the product nonconforming material reports (NCMR) process. An ugly metric is a goal to "reduce NCMRs." While reducing NCMRs is a vision, giving people bonuses for doing so leads to an end to all reporting of NCMRs. That creates a shadow Quality System where everyone knows that the real data is not published. Similarly, a bad metric is to "reduce the rate of repeat NCMRs." That also leads to inaccurate NCMR reporting and increased analysis time to determine which are actually "repeats." A good metric, therefore, is: "Reduce the rate of NCMR escapes from previous control steps," which gives you three areas to measure:

- incoming inspection-found supplier NCMRs

- manufacturing-found supplier or incoming inspection escapes

- customer-found product NCMRs from manufacturing, incoming, or supplier escapes

With three areas to measure, the user has the ability to report issues that should have been caught in a previous step. *People have an incentive to report because the issue is not from their area.*

Some product yield metrics and goals are good but require constant reassessment. An AED company I worked with had a goal to improve product yields to 95 percent. After a couple of months, we achieved that goal in functional product testing but then discovered that the metric did not take into account an offline electrical leakage test. The metric was reset, and the leakage test improved. The metric goal was met again, but then errors occurred in the language-specific programming step. The metric was reset again. An inch-up metric change is actually very effective. An original metric that included all possible issues would have seemed next to impossible to achieve. It would have meant improving the metric from its original 25 percent to 95 percent. But the metric was easier to achieve when we incrementally expanded its scope, keeping resources focused on specific areas to improve.

## CONSILISO TIES IT ALL TOGETHER

Again, there are many worldwide standards and definitions required of medical device manufacturers, but Consiliso ties them all together. That starts when the company is required to have business process documents.

Business processes are composed of procedures, tools, people, and the records they create. People use procedures and work instructions to do the specific work and create records. The best practice is to only define a business process once, and then share that document across business systems. If business systems are not designed properly and organized to share processes, they become the Achilles heel of the company. People work in their own way, and the official records are just window dressing. As a result, product quality suffers. For example, materials acquisition is a common process used across Quality, Clinical, and Finance business systems. Imagine the financial problems in your organization if you had multiple ways to control purchases! I'll discuss the Clinical System and Finance System in the next two chapters.

Figure 3-3 is a simplified view of how business systems overlap each other but not at the policy levels. Most organizations see these systems as separate objects, but they should be viewed as overlapping pyramids/hierarchies.

*Figure 3-3: Overlapping Documentation Pyramids*

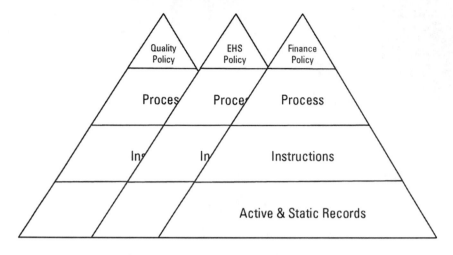

The business process document defines your internal business policies. An example of an internal policy for materials acquisition is that anything less than $3,000 is not capitalized. Anything more than $500 must be signed off by a manager. Anything more than $5,000 must be signed off by the director. A detailed process interaction blueprint (Figure 3-4) defines how the Material Acquisition processes interact with other processes. Note the Material Acquisition process is shown as one gray box in Figure 3-4.

Figure 3-4: Material Acquisition Business Process Detailed Blueprint

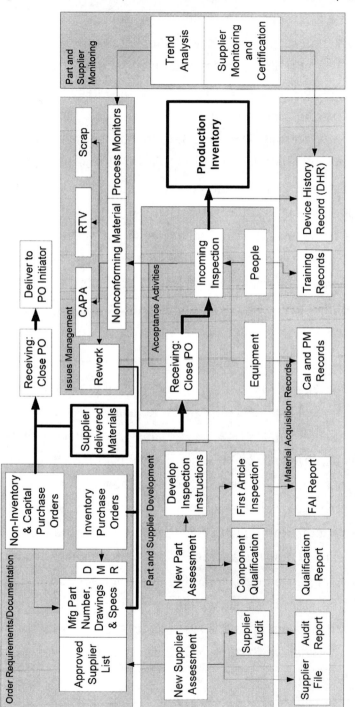

So, in the case of a Material Acquisition process, there are procedures for purchasing, selecting suppliers, qualifying suppliers, receiving materials, and supplier performance monitoring. The business process documents define how those interact and also establish key metrics, tools used to manage the process, and external requirements. With everything in one document—internal policies, interactions, metrics, external requirements, and management tools—it's easy to see how the process works. And the same process works across all products and business systems. Any needed changes most often occur at the procedure level, not at the business process level. Typically, procedures change due to changes in personnel, technology, and products. Business processes, on the other hand, occur across the company, so changes are rarer since they affect nearly everyone.

The goal of a medical device manufacturer is to get product out to the market, and that often includes clinical trials. A Product Quality System in place beforehand helps ensure the success of the clinical trials. One you've designed your business processes, created your business system architecture, and know your Product Quality System, use these components to conduct clinical trials. Using the building analogy: Would you build an entirely different building to begin clinical trials, or just design clinical trials as another floor in the building? Instead of rebuilding an entire Quality System from scratch just for clinical trials, Consiliso lets you design your processes so they grow with different business systems. In the next chapter, I'll discuss the Clinical System in Consiliso and how it manages your clinical trials.

# "OH NO, WE DO THAT"—HAS THIS HAPPENED TO YOU?

Companies often maintain separate documents for expenditure authorizations and purchasing procedures. But that just creates a disconnect that, ultimately, leads to unauthorized purchases.

Ask yourself these questions to see whether you have an adequate Quality System in your company:

1. How many pages are in our Quality Manual?

2. What does our Quality Manual contain?

3. Can I easily find what I need in our Quality Manual?

4. What is our purchasing procedure number?

5. How large a purchase am I authorized to approve?

# CHAPTER 4

# THE CLINICAL SYSTEM

One device company was already growing fairly well before I came on board as the head of the Quality Control department. A few years earlier, it was running a couple of clinical trials, but it didn't quite know what it was doing. The company was still relatively small, only forty people, so when it needed a database for its clinical trials, the Clinical Manager turned to his brother-in-law who created a Microsoft Access clinical database. The clinical trial data was entered into the database, but the database did not meet any of the FDA requirements for clinical data integrity.

Consequently, when the FDA came in to inspect the company, it found that the database was not validated, so the reports from the database were suspect. As a result, the FDA issued an Application Integrity Policy (AIP), which dinged the company for the integrity of the data and information in its submissions to the FDA. Since this occurred outside the Product Quality System, the AIP was issued instead of a warning letter. But, without having control and integrity of its clinical data, the company was in danger of having its submissions rejected.

The problem with databases developed ad hoc is they do not have proven data architecture, and they are subject to constant changes, which makes them hard to validate. The best practice is to use a tool designed for clinical studies.

To resolve the problem, the company built a host of business processes independent of the Product Quality System. There were separate procedures for document control, records management, issues management, auditing, and so on. And nothing was connected to the Product Quality System.

After the AIP was in place, I asked the Clinical Program Manager about the status of all the clinical trials. He could not produce a status report on all the trials, so he just verbally named four active trials. However, there were actually two pending trials, four active trials, and four others in close-out phase. The company had set up a compliance system, but it was incomplete, inefficient, and redundant.

**Consiliso allowed this company to leverage the same functionality utilized for product development programs (which also have set-up, planning, execution and close-out), resulting in a very fast implementation with no need to validate a separate technology tool.**

Without a Consiliso approach to managing clinical trials, you risk having consequences from delayed trial results, to audit findings, to legal actions from the FDA. The FDA performs inspections of clinical trials, and it has many ways to enforce its regulations. Usually, it inspects the sponsoring company, each clinical site (hospital/clinic), or the third-party support groups, such as clinical research organizations (CROs) and diagnostic laboratories that analyze the specimens from the study. Each inspection has the potential to lead to 483 findings, warning letters, or invoking actions to meet the AIP.

After implementing Consiliso, the company had, in one system, everything it needed to know about its trials, from planning, to set-up, to execution, to close-out. Incidentally, it was all done with the same tool used for the Product Quality System, except for the clinical trial-specific database system used to collect data for statistical analysis of trial results. Consiliso allowed this company to leverage the same functionality utilized for product development programs (which also have set-up, planning, execution and close-out), resulting in a very fast implementation with no need to validate a separate technology tool.

## A BUSINESS MANAGEMENT SYSTEM FOR CLINICAL TRIALS

The Clinical Management System is the Consiliso business system for conducting human clinical trials. Every country has regulations for conducting human clinical trials, and there are globally accepted standards. To design a Clinical Management System that takes into account all of these requirements, the first step is to understand the nature and complexity of clinical trials in general.

Clinical trials, or studies, come in all sizes and types. Currently, the National Institutes of Health (NIH) tracks, on ClinicalTrials.gov, more than 160,000 clinical studies with locations in all fifty states and in 185 countries.

Clinical trials are special dispensations that allow medical device companies to test a product on humans in a controlled, in-depth way, before putting it out on the market. Clinical trials minimize the number of people affected if it turns out a product is inadequate for human use. If something goes wrong in a clinical trial involving a smaller sampling of people, the trial is stopped. Without clinical trials, the alternative is to release the product into the marketplace where it could adversely affect thousands.

Smaller companies often conduct only one clinical trial at a time. Start-ups especially may lack the resources to do even a single trial on their own. Instead, they may choose to use a clinical research organization (CRO).

Once the medical device company reaches the size and scope that enables it to conduct its own clinical trials, or potentially multiple trials, then it makes sense to have a Clinical Management System.

A Clinical Management System is essential for integrating the trial planning and approval records, trial database, and site records.

A best practice for managing clinical trial information is to integrate it into a company's existing business processes. The clinical trial project uses the same kind of processes and best practices for managing product development and manufacture. The details and people are dissimilar, but the company information and the processes for analysis, reviews, approvals, and so forth are the same.

However, when most companies begin a clinical trial, they start by creating separate clinical procedures that do not reference any procedures in the Product Quality System. In one company I even saw a clinical procedure on how to select suppliers!

Organizing those procedures and other information on the clinical trial is usually a manual process done with paper documentation or disconnected digital information. Over the years, I have seen clinical trial information organized in file cabinets and three-ring binders, in e-mail folders and on proprietary drives, and on Excel spreadsheets and CDs. Since clinical data determines the outcome of the trial and the FDA must ensure the data used is valid and accurate, the integrity of the data is crucial to a successful clinical trial. When clinical trials are organized haphazardly, without planning or an architecture that promotes better management of the clinical information, then an FDA audit usually finds issues. Also, if clinical trial information is randomly recorded, difficult to track, or impossible to reconcile because it is stored in various file cabinets or on numerous Excel spreadsheets across multiple sites, then the clinical trial is more likely to fail an inspection.

If the trial falls into the "tribal knowledge" trap I discussed in Chapter 2, "Your Business Systems: Then and Now," where the information is sequestered and locally controlled, it is also up to the expertise of your clinical team to determine if it is compliant, and that's a risky approach to ensure success.

## CLINICAL STUDY DOCUMENTATION

When documentation for a clinical trial is in the form of paper and kept in a binder, as it is in many companies, there's certain to be a disconnect in the information flow. The company sponsoring the clinical trial has what is known as a "regulatory binder." These binders include regulatory documents, such as the FDA letter giving the go-ahead to start the trial, the trial plan, clinical protocol, case report forms (CRF), advisory board documentation, and so on. The regulatory binder must contain the *exact same* information at the sponsoring company and at *each* of the clinical sites. The sponsoring company and each of the clinical sites must also have a site binder, which contains site-specific information, such as legal contracts, institutional review board (IRB) records, and clinical monitoring documents and reports.

Imagine all the paper required for a clinical trial with twenty sites or one hundred sites. And all those binders need to match each other *all the time!* Achieving 100 percent compliance at all times is virtually impossible.

With Consiliso, the regulatory and site binders become digital, and the information is organized hierarchically with consistent naming conventions. Using a web-based system, it's just a matter of logging into the master source to access the binders—there are no separate sets of information to become out of sync. The Consiliso clinical trial information architecture is particularly useful when a trial is audited. Even if the clinical sites are required to maintain paper documentation, Consiliso helps ensure everything is in order prior to an audit by having a master source for all documentation: one master source for the truth.

Just as the Finance department has a general ledger (a single place where all numbers in the company merge and are reconciled) clinical trials also need one master source for all the regulatory, protocol, documentation, and other information. With Consiliso, you're able to capture all the information, eliminating errors caused by exceptions.

## LOOK AT IT AS A PROJECT

Each clinical trial is really a project that involves some basic processes and procedures. As a project, it has a beginning and an end, so it is managed as if it had a life cycle.

There are four phases in the clinical trial life cycle: planning, set-up, execution, and close-out as shown in Figure 4.1.

Often, execution is the only phase many people think about, because they are continually asked, "When do we get our first patient?" But there is a considerable amount of work done internally before any external activity begins.

That internal work begins with planning. Proper planning ensures a smooth execution. Set-up follows planning. During the set-up phase, you qualify sites and develop tools to manage the execution phase. Patient

**There are four phases in the clinical trial life cycle: planning, set-up, execution, and close-out.**

interaction occurs during the execution phase, which is usually the longest and most complex part of the study. The close-out phase is, generally, the most ignored of the phases, but there are regulatory requirements for it. Your company could incur delays and extra costs if the study is not closed out properly. The close-out is key to a successful clinical trial, which needs a definitive end, and the data must be used accurately and effectively. Even though the phases of a trial usually run consecutively, they may overlap slightly during the trial. In some trials, one phase may not be completed until the prior phase has been completed.

Regardless of the life cycle phase, all supporting processes operate throughout the trial. The various business processes—Quality Assurance Management, Document Management, Reporting, Training, and Data Management—are already defined in Consiliso.

*Figure 4-1: Clinical Study Phases*

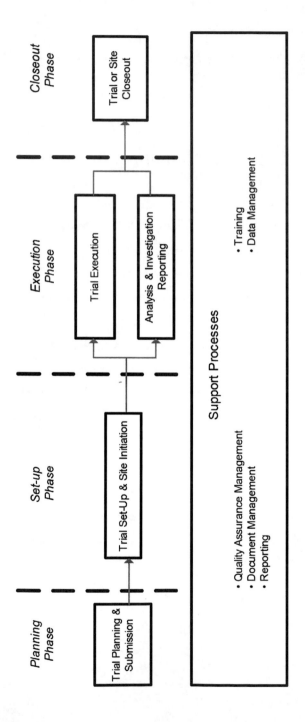

In addition to the business processes, the Clinical System includes some unique documents required to perform a trial. Analogous to the DMR and DHF records required in the Product Quality System, these documents are required for clinical regulatory submissions.

- Case Report Form (CRF)

- Informed Consent (IC)

- Clinical Investigational Plan (CIP)

- Investigator Brochure (IB)

- Manual of Operations (MOO)

Consiliso defines various roles unique to clinical trials in the Clinical System, as well as the process steps, to perform three functions: Trial/Study Management, Site Management, and Data Management. These documentation sets take three personality types to manage. The Study Management personality is characteristic of a project manager, someone who knows how to deal with the Site Management and Data Management people, along with all the other people and components of the project. The Site Management per-sonality is characteristic of someone who is all about people and, ordinarily, wants nothing to do with data. The Data Management personality is characteristic of someone who likes dealing with data, but not so much with people.

Here is a breakdown of the functions and roles for a clinical trial:

- **Trial/Study Management** is the project management for the clinical study. Study Management roles include those of the sponsoring company, contract research organization (CRO), clinical research associate, clinical research coordinator, independent data monitoring committee, and any advisory committees.

- **Site Management** is where the human-subject clinical activity happens. Site Management roles include the subject (patient), the principal investigator (PI), the study coordinator, the independent ethics committee, the institutional review board, a clinical research associate, and a clinical research coordinator.

- **Data Management** is the management of information collected at the sites. Typically, that includes all database development and validation. Data Management roles include those of the sponsoring company, database development personnel, clinical research associate, and clinical research coordinator.

Figure 4-2 shows how Consiliso allocates the process steps among the three functions throughout the four phases of a trial.

*Figure 4-2: Clinical Trial/Study Processes and Phases*

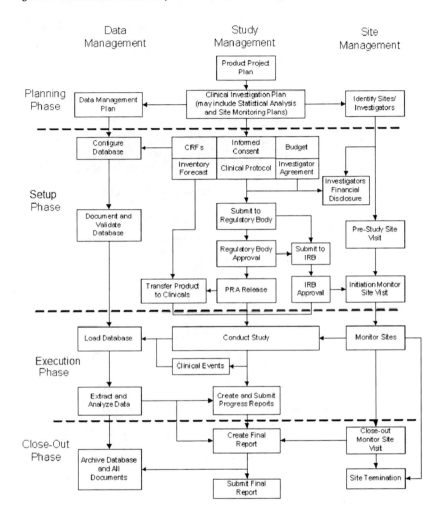

It is a complex task to document everything and keep track of all that goes on in a clinical trial. Consiliso concepts, processes, and tools allow you to electronically create bill of document (BOD) structures in order to establish parent-child relationships for all clinical documentation. That provides easily accessible and search-able clinical study and site documents. A side benefit? It also allows quick identification and retrieval of missing site binder documents and records during clinical site inspections.

The reality is that there are many more components associated with a clinical trial. For instance, manufacturing may build a product specifically for a clinical trial. That's known as a clinical build, and it may also include special labeling. There are also regulatory processes unique to the clinical trial that differ from other products.

Often, other materials purchased for clinical trials are outside the standard materials acquisition for the medical device being tested. For example, you may purchase off-the-shelf headphones (to obscure whether or not the patient is receiving a sham treatment) or sensors (to use in collecting data during the trial). Or, a special piece of equipment may be purchased to perform a particular part of the planned trial tests. That kind of item is tracked differently from the parts used to manufacture the device itself. Yet, they are still part of the clinical trial's device accountability requirements. Similarly, complaints handled during a clinical trial are stored within the clinical trial and adjudicated with the advisory boards, but they must become part of the company's complaint process. Legal contracts, training, order fulfillment—these may all be components of a clinical trial. Yet, if you are thinking from the Consiliso perspective, there is no need to recreate entirely new processes for them.

Consiliso even handles Emergency/Compassionate Use, allowing you to make your product available to a patient whose physician has specifically requested it in an effort to save that patient's life. For instance, physicians can make a special request to use the product if they have patients who are not part of the clinical trial and who may die if they do not get the treatment. That's all part of the *data* included in the device's clinical trial, but the *process* is unique and not documented within a clinical trial protocol.

Figure 4-3 shows how the Clinical Management System's processes interact within the clinical study life cycle and outside it. The box labeled "Clinical Study Life Cycle" in Figure 4-3 encompasses what most companies view as a clinical trial, including the four phases of a clinical trial and the procedures associated with them, along with database training and data management.

Anything can happen with clinical trials on humans. While the trial itself is designed to be very specific, Consiliso accommodates every possible scenario. As I mentioned in Chapter 2, "Your Business Systems: Then and Now," chaos is about controlling the boundaries of processes that may be unpredictable. That's where Consiliso excels.

Integrating clinical trials into your company's business systems provides a level of transparency that ensures completeness. For instance, at the end of a clinical trial, all devices must be accounted for through returns processing. Trial medical devices must be returned into the system, but they must be handled very differently from a standard product return. The trial medical device must be tracked, and that data must connect back to the clinical trial, whether the device is refurbished, relabeled, or destroyed. And yet, those special handling procedures are no reason to create a special returns process—you're still using the same computer system to track the device. The only time you need to change your returns process is to update it to handle clinical returns in time for your company's first clinical trial.

The FDA also wants a considerable number of post-market trials performed these days. "Post-market" is a shorthand term referring to the time after a device receives market approval from the FDA or other regulatory body. Post-market trials further ensure that the product is still safe and works effectively. The two types of post-market studies the FDA may order include 1) post-approval studies, ordered at the time of device approval; and 2) post-market surveillance studies, generally ordered after a device is on the market. All the information gathered by a post-market trial is connected to the original trial through attributed Consiliso projects, events, and documents.

Figure 4-3: Clinical System Process Interaction

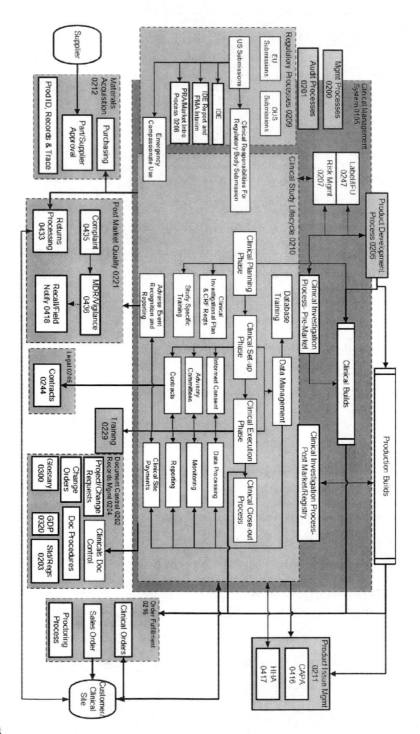

## WITH CONSILISO ON BOARD

Since clinical trials are project-based, Consiliso uses best practices in project and configuration management to make you more efficient. It's a method for helping Lean out parts of the process since that's not something normally done during clinical trials, especially in smaller companies.

With Consiliso, there's no need to "reinvent the wheel" every time you have a clinical trial. Instead, you simply improve processes when a better way is discovered as you manage the chaos.

Plus, Consiliso integrates your clinical trials to your other business processes, making it easier to maintain the integrity of the data. For instance, if a hospital is a clinical site in one of your trials, then that customer record is available for other uses. So, if, say, a future sale occurs, customer information from your Consiliso-designed Product Quality (and Clinical Trial) System is already in the ERP because everything is integrated. Similarly, if a clinical trial physician moves the clinical site during a trial, that information is entered into the master source and the trial continues unhindered.

In short, Consiliso concepts let you create a flexible structure to link everything together.

## "OH NO, WE DO THAT"—HAS THIS HAPPENED TO YOU?

Paper-based clinical trial documentation leaves you open to disconnects. Have patients ever filled out their form and mailed it in to the sponsoring company site and then called in a day later to report a different answer to one of the questions? In a case like that, would the change be communicated back to the sponsor so that their documentation could be corrected? If not, how is it later determined which form is correct? Same thing with lab results: If an issue arose a week after an initial test that resulted in two different lab results, how do you determine which was correct? Consiliso lets you have one consistent information architecture with defined master sources where all information is transparent and integrated. Consiliso is not a tool or a procedure but the blueprint for planning and designing how people do work.

Ask yourself these questions to determine how effective your clinical trial systems are:

1. Do I know the status of all our trials, and do they match ClinicalTrials.gov?

2. What is the status of all our clinical sites?

3. Is there a consistent structure in the naming and numbering of all our clinical trial documents and sites?

4. Do we give each of our project deliverables the same name across our different clinical trials?

# CHAPTER 5
# THE FINANCE SYSTEM

One of the companies I worked with planned to go public, so the Finance group hired a Sarbanes-Oxley (SOX) manager to document the company's financial controls.

We discussed using the Product Quality System documentation to create an integrated approach, but before anything was implemented, the newly hired SOX manager left the company. The company replaced her by hiring a consulting firm, which used eleven of its standard template financial process documents to define more than three hundred internal controls.

External financial auditors then audited the company's SOX documents and deemed them acceptable. The company went public and hired a different internal SOX manager.

Unfortunately, the SOX document control system was stored in the Finance department, and the Quality and Clinical departments each had their own document control systems. Nothing was integrated.

A year later, the company replaced its ERP system, which changed the way the internal controls were implemented and made the SOX process documents useless. The internal SOX manager came to me asking for help in updating the financial process controls for the company. Many of the internal controls were already in the Quality

System documents, but they were not identified as such. So, the solution was relatively simple. Within the existing Product Quality System processes and procedures, we added the tag SOX Control YY-XXX to the documents, thus embedding the SOX controls.

Figure 5-1 shows a list of the internal financial controls identification method originally set up for the company.

Figure 5-1: Internal Controls Identification

| FUNCTIONAL/PROCESS AREA | CONTROL ID FORMAT |
| --- | --- |
| Clinical | CL-XXX |
| Debt management | DM-XXX |
| Entity-wide | EW-XXX |
| Equity management | EM-XXX |
| Financial management | FM-XXX |
| Financial statements | FS-XXX |
| Fixed assets | FA-XXX |
| Income tax | IT-XXX |
| Inventory management | IM-XXX |
| Purchasing (accounts payable) | AP-XXX |
| Sales (accounts receivable) | SM-XXX |

After the update, the purchasing procedure included the following internal control statements:

- Purchase order issuance only by following a procedure of review of the requisition and verification of approvals prior to creation of the purchase order in the ERP system (SOX Control AP–070)

- Quarterly review by purchasing manager of a supplier's direct and indirect purchases to allow for investigation of unusual or unexpected activity (SOX Control AP-050)

- Monitoring by purchasing manager of purchase order activity to ensure manufacturing personnel purchased only from suppliers they were authorized to use (SOX Control AP–130)

- Creation of open purchase order reports by buyer to improve efficiency of follow-up with suppliers on late or back-ordered items (SOX Control AP–190)

To ensure process updates were followed, we implemented a procedural approval rule that the SOX manager had to sign off on any procedure only when a SOX control statement changed.

We then added a metadata field on the procedure document object in the documentation control tool so that all the applicable SOX control IDs were searchable. That feature was similar to the existing FDA and ISO requirements fields. These fields allowed for easy identification of where external requirements and controls were implemented.

At the next financial audit, the auditors loved that the controls were embedded in the operational procedures. Having all of the internal controls in a common set of documents allowed for everyone to be cross-trained. For instance, when purchasing personnel were trained on SOX internal controls, they were also trained on Quality System controls. Rather than having to be trained on multiple documents, they only needed to be trained on one! Also, if something changed, only one document needed revision.

The new system leap-frogged the way in which internal controls were managed and created a state-of-the-art SOX implementation!

It was a world-class system that added visibility to the SOX controls that we implemented without having to completely rewrite current controls, saving the company hundreds of hours.

Today, the preliminary structure of the metadata configuration based on SOX controls is a part of Consiliso (specified in the Consiliso textbook available at Consiliso.com), and it only takes minutes to modify to a company's specific needs.

## FOLLOWING THE MONEY

The Financial Management System seems a little like "going over to the dark side" for anyone not versed in accounting. It is one of the most complex, but also most widely documented, of business systems. Financial management rules differ depending on country, state, and local municipalities, and rules change every year.

The term *financial management* is a misnomer, since it covers more than financial aspects of the business. The people who deal with money have expertise in multiple business processes. The "accounting" group's job is to track the money—that is, deal with the day-to-day transactions and then report on them periodically. From the layman's point of view, they manage the checkbook. "Finance" is the group overseeing the financing of the company, which involves banking, debt, and ownership equity. That includes taking out loans, managing the cash, and dealing with other investments. From the layman's point of view, the finance group manages the mortgage, 401k, and stock portfolio.

Then there are other specialties: tax, capital assets, payroll, equities (company stock), and the oversight processes of internal controls and auditing. All of these roles fall under the oversight of the Chief Financial Officer (CFO). Together, these comprise the

Financial Management System. In small companies, one or two people perform all of these functions.

The Financial Management System is all about financial controls, which means following the money. Every financial transaction (credit or debit) needs an account number assigned to it to determine where it is documented in the general ledger. The general ledger is a complete company history of all the financial transactions using double-entry bookkeeping. Before computers, the general ledger was a book or series of books where transactions were written down, or "posted" in finance speak. With today's computer applications, all transactions are assigned an account code from the chart of accounts and are then posted into database tables used to create required financial and operational reports.

The numbers that comprise those account codes tell something about the transaction. For instance, let's say an account number is made up of three sections: 123-456-789. The first section (123) identifies the department that is creating the charge, such as the Quality, Administration, Legal, IT, or Finance department. The next section (456) identifies what the money is being used for. Is it paying for supplies? For travel and entertainment? For parts to build products? Whatever the purpose, that second section identifies it. The last section of the number (789) matches the budget for a specific purpose. For instance, 789 may be the identifying number for the budget for Project ABC.

So, account numbers posted in general ledger transactions are really just dollar amounts with account metadata assigned to them. That metadata is stored by the company's accounting software or an ERP system that connects all the components associated with the number and then creates the required financial and operational reports.

While some of the processes are finance specific—financial accounting, financial planning, tax management—others are business processes applicable across the company. Capital asset management, cash and debt management, and equity management are all business processes used by Finance but are not specific to financial management. Finance systems are set up by the finance people in the company. No one tells finance people how to set up the rules. They just set them up without consulting anyone else in the company because they have industry-standard rules to follow. Finance doesn't look at other business process key metrics in product quality, sales, marketing, asset management, clinical trials, or other areas of the company. Revenue, profit, losses, having a month-end report—those are the key metrics for Finance. So, while Finance may set up processes in a way that works for their purposes, it's hard to maintain those processes when they affect other areas of the company.

But medical device company executives need more from the numbers. They need to know their metrics, or key performance indicators (KPIs), are being met across the company. If those metrics are not being met, they need to know now, and they need to know why.

By tying everything together into a single architecture, Consiliso lets you see what's happening across the company. It saves you precious hours trying to figure out why the numbers from Finance don't match the numbers from Clinical; why the numbers from Manufacturing don't match the numbers from Quality. Consiliso is the *why* in understanding financial performance. With Consiliso, everyone abides by the same processes and the same operating standards.

## FINANCIAL REQUIREMENTS

Most companies have high-level financial policies and detailed instructions for carrying out transactions with the applicable tool, but there are, customarily, no intermediate-level procedures. That is because the Financial Accounting Standards Board (FASB) maintains the generally accepted accounting principles (GAAP), which comprise a series of financial industry standards (procedures) on how to account for most transactions. Essentially, GAAP are just like Quality System regulations, but they apply to a different set of users.

In addition to GAAP, federal, state, and local government financial regulations exist.

Public companies are also subject to the Sarbanes-Oxley (SOX) Act of 2002, which came about in the wake of the financial crisis that brought down Enron and WorldCom. The SEC enforces SOX and requires executives of public companies to personally certify their company's financial results. The SOX Act also established the Public Company Accounting Oversight Board (PCAOB), a nonprofit corporation to oversee the audits and audit reports of public companies.

While Consiliso is based on the same concepts as the financial side of a business—that there's a place for every transaction—it is designed for anyone to use, not just accountants. Again, Consiliso ties everything together, allowing people in other areas of the company to better understand controls implemented by Finance, which, in turn, produces better quality, consistency, and compliance across a company.

## INTEGRATED TRANSACTIONS

The Finance System in Consiliso also looks at tracking transactions. If you buy, move, build, or sell a part, there's a corresponding financial transaction. Since Consiliso integrates the business processes and transactions, it helps streamline the month-end financial reporting while providing insights into the metrics such as cost of goods, revenue growth, sales territory design, complaint rate, and product line configuration.

Without Consiliso integrating transactions, here's what sometimes happens. Let's say a company sells three product lines. In one month, line A appears to generate $1 million in revenue, line B generates $2 million, and line C generates $3 million. The next month, however, revenues change significantly: Product line A still brings in $1 million, but product line B brings in only $1 million, and product line C brings in $5 million. At first glance, the revenues for product line B appear down, while the revenues for product line C appear to have leaped. But further examination reveals that the product line definitions used by Finance, Manufacturing, and the Complaint groups are different, so the numbers changed because of inconsistent definitions of the product stock keeping units (SKUs).

Consiliso requires consistent definition of product lines across the company, allowing integration of the data from each department. Whether it's Finance, Manufacturing, or Complaints, the product line definition is the *same*; every SKU consistently traces up to one product line in every system or process. That's especially critical when there are hundreds of product lines in a company.

Without consistent configuration of information used by multiple functions, all kinds of disconnects happen. Say, for instance, a company purchases a piece of equipment, and Finance assigns the equipment a capital asset ID tag number. That ID tag lets Finance track the life cycle of the equipment so that it is depreciated over seven years. However, when the piece of equipment needs maintenance, then the Manufacturing group assigns it another tag number.

The same goes for when the equipment is calibrated—the Calibration group gives it another tag. Now the equipment has three tags, which leads to all kinds of disconnected information about that one piece of equipment. I once saw a piece of equipment with five ID tags because every department interacted with it in a different way. Ultimately, Quality became involved because of issues in production caused by the equipment falling out of calibration—Engineering had purchased the machine and tagged it but never told Quality to add it to the calibration program!

With Consiliso, Finance assigns a single asset number to each piece of equipment, and that number is used across the company. Whenever a change occurs to the piece of equipment, the status of that single asset number alters while the company-wide standard change, issue, or event processes occur.

It cannot be overstated: The Finance System is not a stand-alone business system in any company. It directly relates to the other systems in the company. Whether it's the FDA looking to ensure materials were purchased from an approved supplier, or the internal auditor verifying an approval, a Finance System integrates the internal financial controls with the business processes so that answers are just a click away.

## "OH NO, WE DO THAT"—HAS THIS HAPPENED TO YOU?

Medical device companies sell products, and that means they are usually subject to sales tax. Depending on the jurisdiction—city, county, state, ZIP code—that sales tax rate varies, which is difficult to manage as the company grows and expands into other geographies. How do you manage your tax liabilities when your territory crosses so many boundaries?

Consiliso looks at the interaction between the order fulfillment and tax processes to help you better understand various components of a geography, including regulatory approval, clinical reimbursement, taxes, payroll, and people. That's a big help when you are looking to expand.

Ask yourself these questions to determine whether implementing Consiliso could benefit your company:

1. How many ID tags are on a piece of equipment?

2. Does my ERP sales reporting line up with my product lines in Complaints and Regulatory?

3. Did we end up creating separate business processes to manage Sarbanes-Oxley requirements?

## CHAPTER 6

# SEVEN CORE PROCESSES

Back in the early 2000s, ISO 9001:2000 and ISO 13485:2003 added the concept of the "process approach" to those standards. Unfortunately, these ISO standards did not define the need to create a business process document in the documentation hierarchy. At that time, most Quality professionals never embraced the process approach concept. Instead, they were more concerned about the traceability of the standards requirements for their procedures. That led to most companies not defining their specific business processes or their interactions.

In 2016, a South Korean auditor with twenty-five years of experience auditing companies to ISO standards told me that Consiliso was the first time he had actually seen process documents with process interactions. Others also have the same reaction when I start explaining the Consiliso blueprint. One company I worked at was acquired, and the acquiring company came in for a two-day due diligence review. I showed the acquiring company's team my eight-page Quality Manual, which contained a process interaction diagram similar to that shown in Figure 3-1, "Quality System Process Interaction Blueprint" (see Chapter 3, "The Product Quality System"). The team's Quality VP asked me to explain the diagram. I discussed how the process diagram shown in the ISO standard was too simplistic and that my diagram gave context and procedure callouts. I showed her how the parts, products, and information flowed with the arrows between the process blocks. She said it was the most detailed interaction she had seen, and she hoped to find more of the same within the Quality System. The Quality System did not disappoint. Using the Consiliso structures, we loaded *all* of the company's information into an electronic PLM system before the acquisition closed, which enabled a fast and smooth integration.

This chapter covers the seven core business processes required to build an integrated business system, but first let's review the process document concept.

In the previous chapters, I discussed the difference between processes and procedures. The business process document is an overview of how work flows through a company. A process document is a great way to explain to an auditor how a process works. Procedures describe how to *implement* an activity within a process. Procedures are instructions for performing a set of actions, and users must be trained in the steps involved in implementing a procedure. A work instruction is similar to a procedure, but it usually does not require training because it provides step-by-step instructions to a level of detail that allows the user to simply read and perform the task. Some companies even utilize videos demonstrating how to perform a specific task instead of relying on document-based work instructions.

ISO 9001 and ISO 13485 describe the process approach, but they do not give many details on how to implement it. However, ISO 9001:2015 and ISO 13485:2016 now require more definition and management of business processes. Business process documents represent a way to implement the requirements for controlling process policies, metrics, and goals. The process document allows for more focused training of people who need to know how the process works but who do not perform the activities themselves. All management personnel in your company should be trained in all of your process documents so they know how their decisions impact other areas within the company.

---

Consiliso process documents contain the following types of information:

- a listing of policies that contain requirements for the process

- definition of cross-functional roles and required training

- documents referenced/required

    □ policies

    □ procedures

    □ internal operating standards

    □ external standards

- records created

- tools used

- information flow

- decision points

- process objectives and metrics

---

## PROCESSES INCLUDED IN CONSILISO

I have been involved with creating and changing many medical device business processes for over thirty years. After reviewing and designing hundreds of different medical device Quality Systems, I determined that there are more than fifty major business processes used in medical device companies that cross all company functions. At the writing of this book, there are fifty-six processes included in the Consiliso methodology. These process documents contain all the metrics needed for evaluating the company's performance in all functions. Not every company requires all fifty-six business processes. The number any company needs depends on the company size and the type of products manufactured.

A company operates efficiently and compliantly when it knows its business processes, but it is difficult to visualize how they work together unless you have seen how integrated processes (e.g., Consiliso) work.

So, before implementing Consiliso, you must understand what business processes your company requires. Sometimes companies think a new product problem or regulatory requirement means a new business process must be created, and as I've mentioned, companies often design their processes to be independent of each other. But an efficiently run and profitable company integrates its processes and reuses its existing datasets.

Consiliso contains all of the processes any medical device company needs, only requiring slight modifications to match your specific requirements. Even if your company uses a business process that looks as if it does not match one of the fifty-six in Consiliso, it is probably an elective, or subset, of one of the existing processes. For example, Consiliso does not call out a separate nonconforming material process, because it is a subset of the Issue Management Process.

Of the fifty-six processes, I have identified seven core processes that exist in every business management system (e.g., Product Quality, Clinical, Financial). Each management system also has primary and elective processes. Primary processes are those required for business regulations. For instance, you must have a Manufacturing Control process. If you sell products, you also need an Order Fulfillment process. However, you may activate it later if you are still in the development phase.

Elective processes are those that a company may decide to use as it grows or that apply to certain types of devices only. For instance, in the Product Quality System, if your company does not have a capital system, then you do not need the elective processes of Servicing, Installation, and Capital System Lifecycle Management. Or, if your company's products are not required to follow the FDA Device Tracking requirements, then you do not need to activate that process.

---

The systems discussed in the previous chapters—Product Quality, Clinical, and Finance—have the following number of primary and elective processes:

- **Product Quality System** utilizes twenty-six processes: seven core, eight primary, and eleven elective.

- **Clinical System** has twenty-six processes: seven core, one primary, and eighteen elective.

- **Finance System** covers thirty-three processes: seven core, seven primary, and nineteen elective.

Figure 6-1 contains a list of core, primary, and elective business processes used in the Product Quality System.

*Figure 6-1: Quality System Business Processes*

| TYPE | PROCESS NAME |
|------|--------------|
| Core | Management Processes |
| Core | Audit Processes |
| Core | Documentation Control Policies/Processes |
| Core | Standards/Requirements Management Processes |
| Core | Records Management Processes |
| Core | People-Training, Competency, and Awareness |
| Core | Issue Management Processes |
| Primary | Product Development Processes |
| Primary | Product Risk Management Processes |
| Primary | Materials Acquisition and Control Processes |
| Primary | Inventory Control Processes |
| Primary | Manufacturing Process Control Processes |
| Primary | Order Fulfillment Processes |
| Primary | Post-Market Quality (Returns, Complaints, and Trending) |
| Primary | Equipment/Facilities Management Processes |
| Elective | Product Labeling, Marketing Materials, and Artwork Management |
| Elective | Market Introduction/Product Release Process |
| Elective | Product Regulatory Processes |
| Elective | Production Planning Processes |
| Elective | Estimating Processes |
| Elective | Customer Product Management |
| Elective | Installation and Servicing Processes |
| Elective | Capital Systems Lifecycle Process |
| Elective | Import and Export Processes |
| Elective | Information Infrastructure Management Processes |
| Elective | Computer System Validation Process |
| Elective | Customer Communication/Feedback Processes |
| Elective | Device Tracking and Product Registration |

# THE SEVEN CORE PROCESSES

The seven processes that exist in every business management system control all types of information and activities in your company.

1. Management Process

2. Audit Process

3. Documentation Process

4. Standards/Requirements Management Process

5. People Training, Competency, and Awareness Process

6. Records Management Process

7. Issue Management Process

In selecting the seven, I wanted to determine the standards and requirements needed in every business system. I started by looking at the ISO Quality System standards and regulations, ISO14000 for environmental standards, and SOX. Those all called for five core processes: Management, Audit, Documentation, Training, and Records. After looking at configuration management standards and the Capability Maturity Model Integration (CMMI) practices, I then added Standards/Requirements Management. That made for six core processes. Then, as I mapped out all of the processes against the fourteen possible business systems, I realized that the business

**In selecting the seven, I wanted to determine the standards and requirements needed in every business system.**

systems also had one more core process in common: Issue Management.

No matter the business system, there are seven core processes. Once you design these seven business processes to work together, all the other processes your company needs are easy to implement.

> No matter the business system, there are seven core processes. Once you design these seven business processes to work together, all the other processes your company needs are easy to implement. If you are having problems changing your current business processes, then your real problem is your integration of these seven core processes.

If you are having problems changing your current business processes, then your real problem is your integration of these seven core processes.

Using the building analogy, these seven are essentially the utilities/services your medical device company needs to operate the actual structure: water, electricity, internet, sewer, phone, security, and waste management.

Figure 6-2 uses the Audit Process (see "Core Process #2") to show how the seven core processes manage all aspects of any business process. In the next few pages, I will explain each process in more detail.

*Figure 6-2: Business Process Activities and Information Relationships*

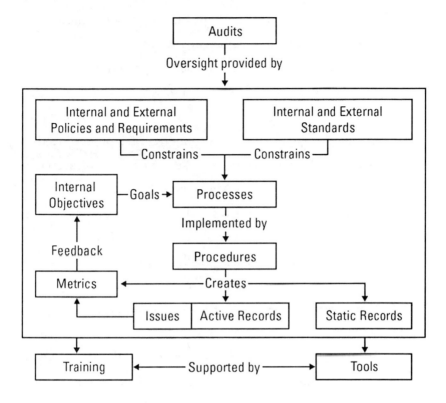

The figure shows how audits provide management oversight. Internal and external policies and requirements, along with internal and external standards, constrain the process; they help to "contain the chaos" in your company. Processes are implemented by procedures. The procedures create active and static records and metrics. Issues found are documented in active records and feed into the metrics. Metrics create feedback for internal objectives. Internal objectives set goals for the processes. Training for users, along with the tools they use, supports the entire process.

As the seven core processes apply: Every business process needs an oversight and control method, and that is where the Management Process and the Audit Process come in. Every process also must be documented, and the Documentation Process covers that need. In the medical device industry, a myriad of ever-changing internal and external standards and requirements constrain activities, so those are managed by the Standards/Requirements Management Process. Every process needs to be supported by a People Training, Competency, and Awareness Process, and every process creates records managed by the Records Management Process. Finally, every process needs to include a feedback loop in order to make continual improvements. That is implemented in the Issue Management Process.

You must set up these processes first, so they are used cross-functionally in all of your business systems. With this common set of processes, you're able to break down the information silos in your company because everything is in the same place, with documentation and training implemented in the same manner. Building your business with an open architecture makes your company transparent. And by designing these seven processes to be flexible and scalable, you enable your people to work within the constraints of the process and empower them to raise issues to improve the process.

For instance, your legal counsel may not want the FDA looking at financial information, and may tell you to keep the Financial Issue Management and Documentation processes separate from the Product Quality Issue Management and Documentation processes. That is shortsighted and a sign of a closed information architecture. It is also bad advice since the FDA does not have the regulatory authority to review financial information. Even if FDA auditors somehow see financial information, they must disregard it. You are more likely to have FDA compliance issues by allowing silos of information and not sharing information with the people who require as much data as possible to make informed decisions.

Consiliso gives you the blueprints to easily set up your seven core processes, along with your primary and elective processes. For instance, it allows you to look at a specific metric daily, such as sales numbers. It also provides you a snapshot of your entire company, allowing you to see the interaction between your processes. So, if a complaint reveals an issue with manufacturing yields, links allow you to see whether they are related. Or, you can see whether your audit findings show why your clinical trials are late. The links allow correlations of data that may explain why your trial spending is higher than expected. Consiliso lets you make connections between datasets, helping you solve problems or ask the right kinds of questions to resolve issues in your company.

Let me break down the seven core processes a little further to help you better understand the value of each.

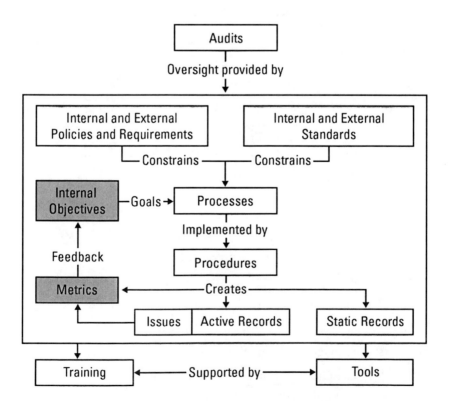

## CORE PROCESS #1: MANAGEMENT PROCESS

The Management Process provides oversight of all of the other business processes in the company. Company leaders need to manage three things: people, products, and processes. If they manage tools, tasks, or times, then they are micromanaging instead of leading.

The Management Process is a standalone process document covering the four major aspects of managing business systems and processes: setting objectives, planning, oversight, and audits. Figure 6-3 shows the interaction between these four activities and the major inputs and outputs of the Management Process.

*Figure 6-3: Management Process Interaction*

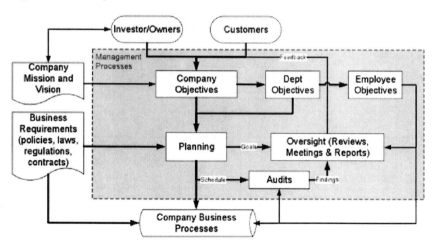

The first requirement for any Management Process is to set the objectives. Objectives are sometimes called your business requirements because they are what you want to achieve—for example, sales growth of 10 percent by year end, a new product launch by December 31, or 30 percent market penetration of a new clinical therapy within two years. Setting clear, defined, and *measurable* objectives is the best way to align the entire company to achieve a goal.

Once the management team has set the objective, plans are formulated for conducting the work needed to achieve that objective. These plans provide the ability to determine if the resources are available to implement the objectives, and they require cross-functional reviews and discussions.

Through oversight, management tracks objectives, plans, and the statuses of the business processes in the company. Well-defined business processes have documented owners and KPIs. Better company performance happens if oversight is consistent across all processes.

Every business process optionally utilizes audits (see "Core Process #2"). Audits are a systematic and independent examination of activities and documents to determine whether activities were conducted and the data was recorded, analyzed, and accurately reported according to released procedures and applicable regulatory requirements. If the audit focuses on one area, product, or activity, it is an investigation, not an audit.

The Management Process also adds value to the Quality System Management Review by compiling the data and letting you see everything in one place, at any time. No need for specialized review meetings with each department just to see how your company is operating. Consiliso's integration and standardization concepts let you quickly review everyone's metrics and objectives using consistent methods. Gone are the daylong Quality System Management Reviews!

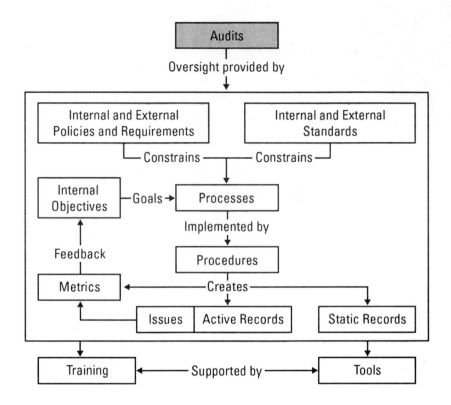

## CORE PROCESS #2: AUDIT PROCESS

Many types of audits occur in any company, but do you manage all of them to provide the maximum benefit? Ask yourself: What do they entail? How often are they conducted? Who participates in them? How are they done with complete confidence? The Audit Process enables an independent review of business processes or activities so that management may confidently make decisions using data generated by that activity/process.

As with all business processes, the Audit Process provides consistency in operations. I have been at companies that had seven separate kinds of audits, and every group conducted its audits differently! I've also been at companies that ended up having the same audit performed three times by three different groups. How do you, as an executive, know whether the numbers are accurate? How do you get the information you need? By setting up the Audit Process as a core process, you eliminate redundancies, provide transparency, and have access to the answers you need, when you need them.

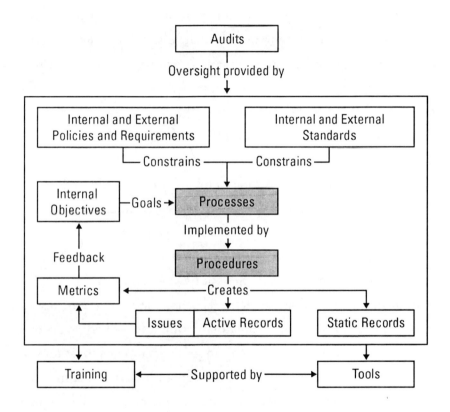

## CORE PROCESS #3: DOCUMENTATION PROCESS

What is your definition of documentation? Is it the activity that your Documentation group performs to release documents for the production floor? Is it any controlled document? Or, is it any document that gets signed?

Consiliso defines documentation as "formally released information needed to run your company."

The Documentation Process is about creating, storing, linking, numbering, and approving document *and* part objects. The ability to easily find and control all of the documentation in your company represents a competitive advantage. Your company should have one consistent methodology for controlling all the information generated.

Half the problems with documentation stem from people not knowing which document to use—which version is the right version? I have seen engineers create engineering reports with no identification or revision numbers. Those reports were then submitted to the FDA. When the FDA asked about the submitted report, it referred to the report as "document number TBD, revision XX." An unreleased document had been sent to the FDA, which now wanted verification of what was reported! It was a little embarrassing, to say the least.

The Documentation Process defines when and what kind of approval is needed, where documents are stored, how they are named and numbered, and so on—all the basic requirements to ensure consistency throughout your operations. Documentation becomes a problem when bottlenecks occur because the wrong controls are implemented to meet the regulatory requirement. Have you ever heard that *all* the people who sign company documents must review/approve *all* documents, per the FDA's regulations? That is simply not true. The FDA regulations state: "Each manufacturer shall designate an individual(s) to review for adequacy and approve prior to issuance all documents."[9]

Did you know that your engineers spend half their time looking for information that someone else in your company already found or created? At one company, I had two drafters creating drawings, and

---

9    21CFR820.3 (v), CFR - Code of Federal Regulations, U.S. Food & Drug Administration Title 21, vol. 8 (April 1, 2016), accessed May 3, 2017, https://www.accessdata.fda.gov/scripts/cdrh/cfdocs/cfCFR/CFRSearch.cfm?fr=820.40.

they needed to share 3-D models among themselves and the other engineers. When they left the company, I replaced them both with one drafter. The new drafter standardized file naming and instituted controls with a product data management (PDM) system. The one drafter did the work of the other two. Was he more highly skilled? No, he just spent much less time looking for misplaced 3-D files. When only one person creates information and then uses it, that individual is more productive than two people having to find each other's information. Since most companies cannot have one person doing all of the work, you need to establish strong controls, but they must be easy to use. The Consiliso Documentation Process provides the correct level of control to increase productivity and ensure compliance.

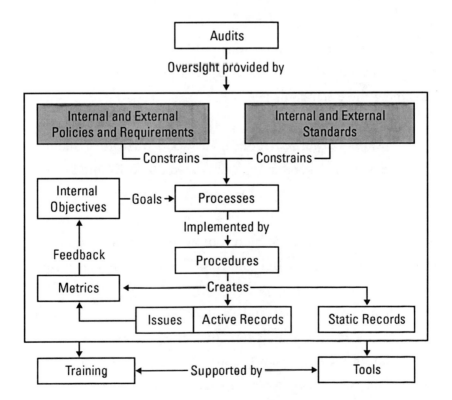

## CORE PROCESS #4: STANDARDS/ REQUIREMENTS MANAGEMENT PROCESS

The Standards/Requirements Management Process is about the requirements the company follows in its products and business processes. These include: internal policies, standard practices, external standards, state and federal laws and regulations, and laws of other countries. The ability to easily find, use, and change standards and requirements in your company's projects, products, and processes eliminates wasted efforts and the risk of noncompliance when requirements change.

When your company has a new medical device requiring regulatory approval, you must meet many external standards to design, build, and test the product. To get through the FDA's submission process faster, use the FDA's defined consensus standards. If a consensus standard applies to your product and you don't follow it, then you must justify to the FDA why you employed another method. Managing these standards is a part of the Standards/Requirements Management Process.

Consiliso categorized more than 1,600 predefined standards, laws, and regulations pertaining to any medical device and in various geographies. Just search by area or product type, and the standards are all there for you! That eliminates a big part of the approval battle, which is simply trying to figure out which standards apply. This curated information, available on Consiliso.com, is also organized by the type of standard.

When it comes to the standards, laws, and regulations of medical device manufacturing, companies don't always know what they don't know. But with Consiliso, you don't have to know, because it is all together in one place and continuously updated as laws, regulations, standards and guidance documents evolve.

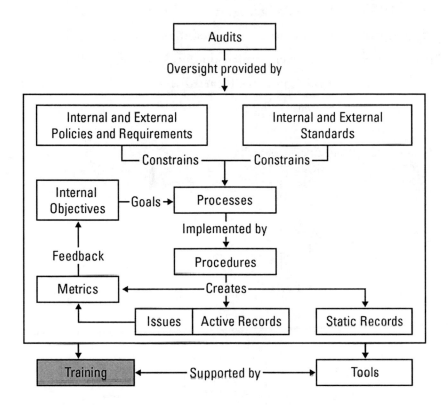

## CORE PROCESS #5: PEOPLE TRAINING, COMPETENCY, AND AWARENESS PROCESS

Back in the 1980s, I had a discussion with a Human Resources (HR) manager about a project to update all of the company's job descriptions. The company had a four-drawer file cabinet filled with job descriptions in need of analysis and reorganization. Actually, "reorganization" is an understatement. There were more job descriptions in that file cabinet than there were people in the company! This common problem occurred because any manager needing to hire someone had to submit a job description in order to post the job opening. Managers simply copied previous job descriptions and added or subtracted information. There was no standardization or revision control

125

of the job descriptions. As I talked to the HR manager about the procedural training requirements, I realized that the hiring, performance reviews, and training were a plan-do-check-act (PDCA) cycle (see Figure 6-4). After this epiphany, I started seeing closed-loop business processes in other areas of the company.

*Figure 6-4: Employee Competency PDCA*

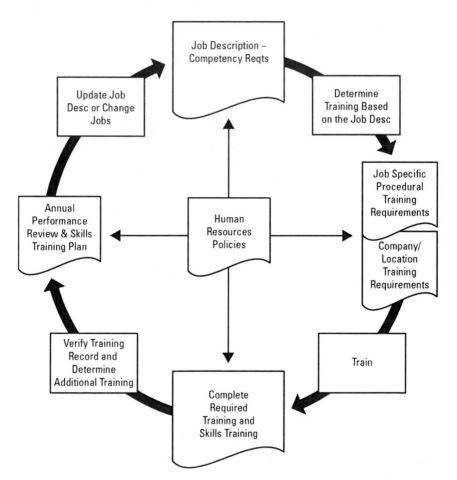

The ideal workforce is one that is happy and stable. That comes from a company having the ability and capability to hire the right people, have them learn the job, and then challenge them. The

People Training, Competency, and Awareness Process is necessary for all business systems. Training is not just people reading about a new procedure and then signing a document to confirm that they "read and understood" it. The regulatory requirements for medical device makers won't let you get away with that level of training for very long.

Training must be based on the job description. People should complete the skills training they need for their job. Then, a year later, implement an annual performance and skills training plan. The job description might be updated at that point—that's the competency-awareness piece of the requirement. Conducting that annual performance and skills-training plan helps you see if your people are still in the right job for their skill sets. Do they need additional training? If so, did they complete it? If they're doing well, should they be promoted? If so, then guess what—they need training for their new responsibilities.

In many companies, the job descriptions and training are disconnected, completely separate. In Consiliso, everything is connected because it's all related.

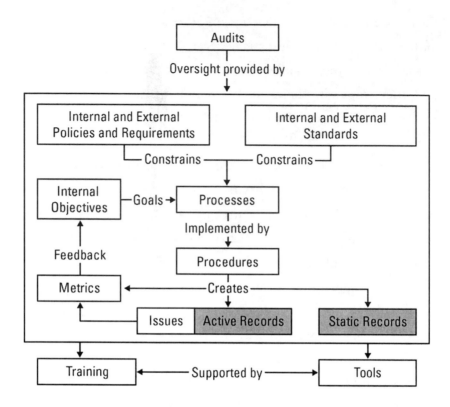

## CORE PROCESS #6: RECORDS MANAGEMENT PROCESS

The Records Management Process makes it easy to find and control all of the records in the company. Every business process creates records, so the Records Management Process is fed by outputs of all of the other business processes. Most records are accessed once or twice after being completed, but they could be needed hundreds of times.

The Records Management Process is the last one that companies usually think about until experiencing either a recall or lawsuit. But implementing this process early on, and correctly, could save you a huge headache.

I remember talking to a supplier of a component for a high-voltage resistor that went inside a defibrillator. I was the component engineer, and I had some questions for the supplier regarding where the records were stored. He informed me that, after a build, the records were kept in a file drawer for that build: the top drawer of a three-drawer file cabinet, because that's where new records were kept. The file cabinet was not fireproof or waterproof, so the files weren't protected from damage.

After a year, the records were moved down one drawer to make room for new records to be placed in the top drawer. "What happens after three years when the file cabinet is full?" I asked, to which the supplier replied, "I just throw the old records away to make room for more." The very serious problem with the supplier's records system was that the devices we built lasted longer than three years, and if any of them out in the market failed, we would need the build records for *all* the components.

Part of Records Management in Consiliso requires defining the various types of records you have in your company and how long you want to keep them. The definitions for records storage are based on a variety of laws and regulations across the business. For instance, tax records must be stored seven years, employee-hiring records need to be kept for three years, and records for medical devices—such as an implanted pacemaker—might need to be kept for fifty years or more.

Records Management also defines access. In Consiliso,

Having a Consiliso-designed Records Management Process means you run a much lower risk of not knowing the location of, not having access to, or accidentally destroying needed information.

only three types of record access exist: public, confidential, and restricted. Public records require no special controls. Records defined as confidential are shared within the company and anyone in the company may view them. Since most companies control access to their facilities, confidential records are often stored in unlocked file cabinets or company network locations. But controls are put in place when these records are shared outside the company or destroyed. Restricted records have an additional level of control (either locked cabinets/rooms or electronically controlled access) to prevent unauthorized viewing. Having a Consiliso-designed Records Management Process means you run a much lower risk of not knowing the location of, not having access to, or accidentally destroying needed information.

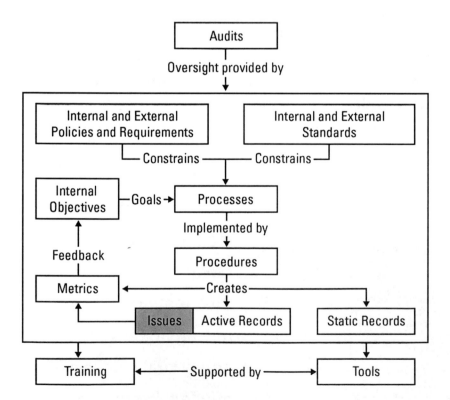

# CORE PROCESS #7: ISSUE MANAGEMENT PROCESS

The ability to track, investigate, resolve, and trend all of the issues occurring in your company drives continuous improvement.

The Issue Management Process covers dealing with problems that inevitably arise. That includes everything from accidents, to IT help-desk requests, to in-house product quality failures, to complaints from the field. Issue Management is a highly disciplined activity, and every step must be tracked in some cases, based on external regulations. But all issues go through the same basic workflow, so best practices are reusable for issues occurring in any part of the company.

The most serious issue any medical device business experiences is a product complaint. Going back to the basics, the FDA definition of a complaint is: "any written, electronic, or oral communication that alleges deficiencies related to the identity, quality, durability, reliability, safety, effectiveness, or performance of a device after it is released for distribution."[10]

A simplified version of that definition is that you are dealing with a complaint if:

- someone is unhappy because your device did not meet expectations;

- your device has not worked as expected; or

- a patient has an unplanned surgery or medical treatment related to your device.

These definitions are very broad, and they give the FDA a lot of leeway in determining what needs to be tracked as a complaint. In addition, the FDA defines what you must report when a serious event

---

10    21CFR820.3 (v), CFR - Code of Federal Regulations, U.S. Food & Drug Administration Title 21, vol. 8 (April 1, 2016), accessed May 3, 2017, https://www.access-data.fda.gov/scripts/cdrh/cfdocs/cfCFR/CFRSearch.cfm?fr=820.3.

occurs, in what's known as an MDR (Medical Device Reporting per 21 CFR 803). The FDA tracks all MDRs in its Manufacturer and User Facility Device Experience (MAUDE) database, which is searchable by anyone on the FDA.gov website. In June 2014, the FDA allowed direct downloads of publicly available FDA data through an open portal (https://open.fda.gov/). That allows anyone—including your competitors—to see and analyze your most serious complaints!

Yet, accessing and analyzing a company's MDR data does not always give you the right perspective. For instance, an implantable electrical device company had a policy that any battery depletion was an MDR-reportable complaint. Battery depletion was a process completely managed by the patient and physician, but it met the requirement of a complaint and an adverse event. So, the conservative approach was to report all battery depletions—tens of thousands per year. Since competitors' policies were to not report standard battery depletion as an MDR, comparing failure trends on MAUDE between companies resulted in wrong conclusions.

The Consiliso Issue Management Process covers any type of issue in the company by just changing a few attributes and access privileges, but keeping the same workflows. The Issue Management Process is also used to respond to regulatory submission deficiencies, SOX findings, employment investigations, insider trading investigations, accident investigations, hacking events, and even response to concerns raised by the public.

Issue Management in Consiliso lets you capture all the data pertaining to each problem to help you better prioritize and resolve the issue. The critical ones, obviously, must be solved first, which is what ISO standards require. With everything captured in one location, you have the transparency needed to triage and prioritize the higher-priority issues first while tracking every detail of the issue and its resolution. Without prioritizing your issues, you are exposing your company to more risk.

Most issue types are sub-processes that allow for immediate corrective actions without needing to go into excessive details or tracking. These issue sub-processes create a risk-based way of triaging issues because they allow simple ones to be dealt with in a small, functional area of the company, while the most serious and systemic issues are then managed across the company as CAPAs.

How a company manages its CAPAs reveals how serious it is about solving problems. I have seen a billion-dollar medical device division have only a couple of CAPAs a year and a $5 million start-up company manage twenty CAPAs a year. Almost any time there is a product field issue, there should be a CAPA. Inputs (processes and sources) to issues lead into the CAPA feeder systems (i.e., issue sub-processes), which allows for the identification of problems that should initiate a CAPA.

The process interaction blueprint in Figure 6-5 shows how typical feeder systems become different types of issues and, possibly, CAPAs.

Figure 6-5: Issue Management Process Interaction Blueprint

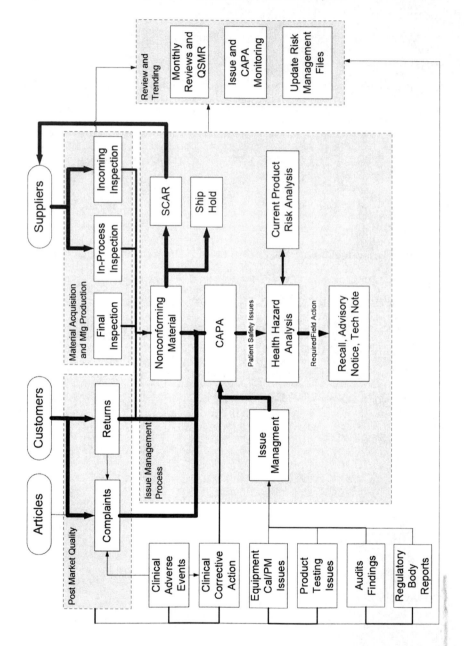

General issues, complaints, and nonconforming material reports (NCMRs) feed into CAPAs, and patient-safety issues must be assessed to determine if a field action is needed. The blueprint shows how NCMRs feed into Supplier Corrective Action Requests (SCARs) and back to suppliers. All the data from the Issue Management Process is then used for reviews and trending.

By now, the complexity of your medical device operations should be apparent. When your core processes operate as islands—Management; Audit; Documentation; Standards/Requirements Management; People Training, Competency and Awareness; Records Management; and Issue Management—everything is disconnected, and problems arise. With Consiliso, everything is connected; everything is in one place.

## "OH NO, WE DO THAT"—HAS THIS HAPPENED TO YOU?

When the FDA comes in for an audit, auditors usually look at many aspects of any issues the company experienced. For instance, let's say the FDA auditor asks for the number of returns your company had in a year, how many of those returns were complaints, how many were investigations, and how many investigations became CAPAs.

If your company operates with separate systems, then you must look into each of those systems for answers. Even if you find the answers, how do you ensure the numbers line up between the various systems? When everything is organized using the Consiliso methodology, you quickly find answers, and all your information correlates. Traceability becomes inherent when it is all in one tool. Otherwise, you operate with islands and disconnects.

Ask yourself these questions to see whether your company has problems with its core processes:

1. Do our systems feed from one to the next, or do they stand alone and only one person knows what is going on in each of these islands of information?

2. Do issues travel between systems?

3. Do we duplicate information?

CHAPTER 7

# FACING AN AUDIT OR INSPECTION? HAVE NO FEAR

Back in 2006, I was brought into a company to remediate an FDA warning letter. Six months before I arrived, the company underwent an FDA inspection, and its Quality group was unprepared for what was ahead. The group had never been through the FDA's Quality System Inspection Technique (QSIT), which starts with an examination of the company's complaints-and-returns handling and then moves into nonconformance and CAPA processes. The inspection reviews how the issues are captured, tracked, reported, and then how corrective actions are either taken or not. The inspectors use statistically relevant sample sizes to analyze the data themselves. They want to see if the company analyzed the data correctly.

Normally, the QSIT inspection takes about five days, but in this particular instance, it stretched to three weeks. Since the Quality group had not been through a QSIT before, it did not understand the kind of information the inspector wanted. To the inspector, that also meant that the Quality group did not understand its own Quality System. As a result of the group's inability to find answers quickly, the inspector lost confidence in the company. He thought that if people on the Quality team could not adequately answer inspection questions, the Quality System itself was inherently flawed. That led to a 483, indicating there was a systematic problem in the company. What happened in that company—and it is indicative of most medical device companies—occurred because the Product Quality Systems were patched together instead of being designed to work together.

As I discussed in Chapter 1, "Consiliso: What It Is, What It Means to You," the way most companies organize their paper-based Quality System means that the inspection requires many people working in concert to answer all of the questions posed by the auditor. The inspection is usually set up with a couple of people interfacing with the inspector and then a "backroom" with a team of people collecting the documents/records the inspector requests.

But inspectors want timely access to required Quality System information. If it takes a day to retrieve thirty complaint files for the inspector to review, the inspector may question how quickly your company is able to handle complaints. If you do not use a robust process for tracking, trending, and resolving issues, get ready to sweat when the inspector starts asking questions about how your process works.

Defining your Quality System business processes is absolutely essential so that all employees know what is required of them. Designing your business processes to be audited saves the company time and money. Note: This does not mean your procedures should be written for the auditors; they need to be

**A properly designed Quality System that is set up for audits and inspections will also be easy for users to navigate.**

written for the users. A properly designed Quality System that is set up for audits and inspections will also be easy for users to navigate.

If you have a Consiliso-designed Quality System, then virtually all the data that an inspector wants is at your fingertips—no "backroom" needed.

## FDA INSPECTIONS

Companies must follow laws and regulations as they perform their business. Some companies do not follow the rules because they do not know they exist, or they blatantly disregard them. Noncompliant practices may work for a short while, but in the long term, they will always backfire. The regulating body will eventually show up for an inspection, and the company must comply or face fines and recalls and, possibly, be shut down.

To clarify, I use the terms *audit* and *inspection* somewhat interchangeably. Here's why:

- The term *audit* defines an internal review of processes through a sampling of procedures and records.

- The term *inspection* refers to what an external regulatory body most often calls an audit.

Both of these activities entail reviewing business process records according to internal and external requirements and verifying that people follow the processes. The verification step involves interviewing people and reviewing applicable records. The main difference between them is that internal audits are planned and scheduled and external inspections are not.

Companies in the medical device industry (or in any regulated industry) dread the regulatory body coming in to carry out an inspection. That is when all the company's work is put to the test.

Depending on the regulating body, the results of the inspection may range from no issues found, to actions requiring a written response, to fines (usually for environmental, health, and safety issues), to official actions. Getting an official action from the FDA may lead to new products being held up in the submission cycle, products being taken off the market, seizure of adulterated product, large fines, and people being banned from the industry and/or going to jail. These last actions are the worst-case scenario, but it does happen!

Since the FDA inspection is one of the most difficult to manage, the rest of this chapter focuses on techniques that help these inspections go smoothly. Other nonproduct regulatory bodies, such as the EPA, carry out inspections based on the permits assigned to the company. OSHA performs inspections based on a periodic cycle or if there are reportable incidents. These inspections are similar to Quality System audits, but they focus on specific areas in other business processes. State/provincial regulating bodies initiate these inspections, not federal agencies. Other countries such as Japan, South Korea, and Brazil also do periodic inspections. Inspections are either based on a regular schedule or a new product submission, or they are triggered by adverse events and complaints.

> Regardless of the inspecting body, by applying Consiliso principles of integrated business process controls, the inspectors will find the same level of documented compliance present in processes subject to FDA regulations.

Regardless of the inspecting body, by applying Consiliso principles of integrated business process controls, the inspectors will find the same level of documented compliance present in processes subject to FDA regulations.

The FDA is required by law to inspect FDA-registered medical device manufacturers every three years. Depending on the type of product, the FDA is also required to conduct specific pre-approval and post-market inspections. The level of inspection directly relates to the FDA's product classification system: Class I comprises low-risk products, such as cotton swabs and bandages; Class II comprises medium-risk products, such as balloon catheters and MRI machines; Class III comprises high-risk products requiring premarket approval (PMA), such as implantable pacemakers and defibrillators. Other countries also have varying inspection classes.

Normally, a Class I or Class II manufacturer only sees an inspection every three years. I worked at a Class III implantable manufacturer that underwent twenty-seven inspections in a three-year time frame due to serious compliance issues. The FDA may combine these inspections, such as doing pre- and post-market inspections for various products during the same visit.

## THE AUDIT/INSPECTION

There are hundreds of articles, papers, and books on how to manage an external regulatory body inspection. Most papers discuss the legal limits for controlling the inspection, but inspectors seldom push the boundaries. Good auditors do not want to nitpick the auditee but instead determine if issues are systemic or one-off. Audits often uncover issues that are repetitive, and few things during an inspection waste everyone's time more than having to answer what seem to be multiple issues separately when a single change to the underlying cause would resolve everything.

Here are a few tactics to help your audit team when it comes to an audit/inspection:

**Employ the Golden Rule**. Treat inspectors as you would like to be treated. Don't do as one company that hated inspections did: It set up a table for the inspector at the back of a warehouse where it was so cold, she had to conduct the entire inspection wearing a coat.

**Allow room to breathe**. Give yourself and the inspectors enough working space to be comfortable. Use an out-of-the-way conference room but not one that feels like a closet. Conduct an FDA inspection in a conference room that is more isolated than the one used for the ISO audit. This allows fewer distractions, but it should be comfortable. And have a window—you do not want to feel you are in a box; audits are stressful enough!

**Be courteous**. FDA inspectors will not accept food, but other auditors will, so bring in some refreshments. That small token of courtesy helps you build a cordial relationship with the inspector versus an adversarial one.

**Have the right number of people for the audit**. Have at least two people in the room—one to work directly with the auditor, and the other to gather information or assist in taking notes. Also, do not have more than two people per inspector, or the room will become too noisy or busy.

**Use people who add value, not just hosts**. It takes a special kind of person to know how to work with an inspector during an audit, someone who is more than just a host. People in the room should add value to the inspection. The person working directly with the auditor should be someone who knows how to answer questions honestly and succinctly. Have people who understand how your systems work and who know how to find and interpret information.

**Know when to keep quiet**. When the FDA inspector reads through records, it is extremely quiet for minutes on end. Do not talk during this time. The less said the better. If you have your laptop, communicate with your team, maintain the audit record, and keep up with other tasks during this awkward silence. The last thing you want is for someone in the room to say something they shouldn't, such as, "Well, that's always been a problem for us."

**Look for ISO audit results**. A good ISO auditor will conduct a SWOT analysis of your company that should include identifying

- **S**trengths: your company's best practices

- **W**eaknesses: general areas where your company needs systemic improvements

- **O**pportunities: areas where other processes in the company could be leveraged to make improvements

- **T**hreats: concerns from other areas of the company that could cause problems in the future

**Ask about audit findings**. At the end of a day, always ask if any issues were found. The auditor may not tell you but usually does. Once the audit is over, results are discussed in a closing meeting. If there are no findings, there may not be a meeting.

With regulatory bodies, it is tough to refute findings, but you can work to close them before they are written. With other auditors, it is okay to refute findings if they are interpreting the regulations in a manner that is not in line with your business process, products, or regulatory requirements. Often, a finding that is not per regulation or guidance document is changed to an observation.

## DEALING WITH FINDINGS

Once the inspection or audit is complete, you may have to respond to findings. For non-FDA audits, the findings are customarily broken into three types: nonconformance, observation, or areas for improvement. In an FDA inspection, if you have no findings, great for you! The FDA will not give you a 483, and your company's compliance status is now "No Action Indicated" (NAI). The FDA sends you a complete establishment inspection report (EIR) in about four to eight weeks.

If you receive a 483, it lists the findings that require a timely written response. These 483 findings are symptoms the FDA sees as systemic problems with your business processes, and the FDA wants your response to the findings to be about rebuilding your processes to make them more robust. If you only respond that you will fix the specific issue and retrain, you will most likely receive a warning letter.

The warning letter is the FDA's next enforcement tool to entice companies to fix their business processes to meet the regulations. A note of caution: As I mentioned in Chapter 6, "Seven Core Processes," the findings of the FDA are made public on its website, FDA.gov. So, whether you want your business (and failings) known or not, they are out there for everyone—the public as well as your competitors—to view. When the FDA moves through its succession of enforcement tools—consent decrees, seizures, and civil and criminal prosecutions—the findings are all posted online.

For instance, as I was putting together this chapter, health care giant Abbott Laboratories' long struggle with one of its pacemakers came to a head in the form of a warning letter, which was posted on the FDA website. A year earlier, Abbott had battled claims of risks involved with the pacemaker in question, including claims that it was hackable. Of course, there was considerable media coverage of the warning letter, including a Dow Jones article that stated, "Analysts said the FDA's letter, which describes the company overlooking or omitting early signals of product defects or vulnerabilities, could hurt Abbott's reputation among cardiologists."[11]

Contrary to what some companies may believe, the FDA desires companies to continually improve. The FDA wants companies to make great products, since those products affect humans, and it ensures companies stay on track through compliance.

In fact, as I write this book, medical device companies may soon be motivated to continually improve their processes. The FDA is looking at a maturity model for medical device companies that may permit those companies that stay on the path of continuous improvement to benefit from fewer inspections.

If you have Consiliso in your corner, you are on top of the maturity model, and that may soon weigh in your favor when it comes to audits and inspections.

**The FDA is looking at a maturity model for medical device companies that may permit those companies that stay on the path of continuous improvement to benefit from fewer inspections.**

---

11    Dow Jones News Service, "FDA warns on Abbott's St. Jude pacemakers and defibrillators," *Twin Cities Pioneer Press*, April 13, 2017, accessed May 4, 2017, http://www.twincities.com/2017/04/13/fda-warns-on-abbotts-st-jude-pacemakers-and-defibrillators/.

## AUDIT/INSPECTION WITH CONSILISO

Consiliso lets you bulletproof integrated business systems and processes that cover all the types of inspections and audits that you could experience, and keep warning letters from appearing at your door.

Consiliso also saves you time and costs. For instance, if it takes eight people to support a three-week FDA audit with a backroom set-up, that's actually twenty-four weeks of full-time equivalent (FTE) pay—maybe $100,000 in salary alone. Add to that the time it takes to prep for the audit, and that also may add up to one year of FTE. With Consiliso, audits are reduced to a matter of hours, and fewer personnel are tied up running down information. By making it possible for fewer people to provide answers in under a day via Consiliso, you could feasibly save as much as 90 percent of the costs of a paper-based inspection.

Consiliso Quality Systems are designed to need fewer people to manage an FDA QSIT inspection. With the entire Quality System accessed within one or two software tools, all requested data is instantly available, and the inspector reviews the data live in the system. Quality System data is designed and organized so that it is *always* properly reviewed and correct, so there are no worries about showing the inspector the information directly. The ability to display the information instantly also helps in developing trust with the inspector, who won't feel the need to dig further because the system clearly proves that the information viewed is "clean." With no paper files to review, there is no danger of random Post-it notes or handwritten changes appearing, thereby disrupting the inspection and, potentially, even leading to a nonconformance, observation, or worse!

In other words, with Consiliso, there is no need to fear an audit or inspection by the FDA or other regulating body. Everything you need is there, easily retrievable by your audit team, and ready to provide answers in minutes.

## "OH NO, WE DO THAT"—HAS THIS HAPPENED TO YOU?

Some companies carry out mock audits to see how long it takes to retrieve information. One company even created a database to track how many records had to be pulled, where they were located, how long the whole process took, and so on. That mock audit helped the company perform the live one smoothly. The only problem was that, once the audit was over, the structure created was tossed aside instead of being used in other areas of the company. Since it wasn't incorporated into the company's systems, the company had, ultimately, engaged in wasteful compliance.

If you have a Consiliso-designed Quality System, then virtually all the data that an inspector wants is at your fingertips—no "backroom" needed. And since your systems and processes are inherent in Consiliso, they are used wherever needed throughout the company.

How prepared are you for an audit or inspection? Ask yourself these questions:

1.  Is our inspection point person a host, or do they add more value because they know what's required?

2.  When was our last FDA inspection? (If it was more than three years ago, expect the inspectors to be showing up any moment.)

3.  Are we ready for our next FDA inspection?

# CONCLUSION

The maturity level of a company is based on the capability, scalability, and integration of its business processes. Consiliso blueprints give you a "medical device company in a box," helping move your organization to the highest level of maturity.

Consiliso sets industry-wide, world-class standards for medical device maker compliance documentation work and business processes. It acts as the framework to "contain the chaos" involved in maintaining compliance, allowing you to focus on what your company does best: designing, building, and selling quality medical devices.

> **Consiliso blueprints give you a "medical device company in a box," helping move your organization to the highest level of maturity.**

Since it is scalable, Consiliso works for companies of any size. Companies I've implemented it in include a thirty-person start-up, a $60 million public company, a $200 million privately held company, and a division of a multibillion-dollar corporation.

Consiliso lets your company experience added valuation right away. One start-up CEO reported that with only one-quarter of Consiliso concepts implemented, the company's market value was up 1 percent. In fact, with Consiliso, small companies often increase their market value by up to 5 percent because an acquiring company can easily locate all the intellectual property and product documentation, resulting in less integration work. Literally, one or two people using Consiliso can integrate all the information between two companies in a week—that's versus having a team of people taking months to years to integrate a paper-based system where nothing seems to match.

> One start-up CEO reported that with only one-quarter of Consiliso concepts implemented, the company's market value was up 1 percent. In fact, with Consiliso, small companies often increase their market value by up to 5 percent.

And Consiliso's provision of industry-wide standardization adds value for both companies in an acquisition—the acquirer and the acquired. Small-device makers are more attractive to global corporations, and isn't that the end goal: to get your medical device into the bigger market where it helps people around the world? That's something start-ups are seldom able to do on their own.

But change takes the commitment of everyone in the company, and that starts at the top. Employing a new system such as Consiliso relies on acceptance and ownership by the executive team. Why operate with paper-based or disparate systems when blueprints such as Consiliso exist? And yet, I have seen companies in the discovery stage of a lawsuit spend $100,000 on paralegals to do nothing more than search for documents and then create three pallets of copies. Why? Especially when Consiliso, implemented with a PLM system, generates a report that extracts everything needed on a product in *minutes*.

Too often, Quality groups view themselves as product quality control, or a police group, only involved in enforcement. But who's running your Quality System? Using the building analogy, your Quality group is the builder or maintenance provider, not the architect. They may say paper-based, spreadsheets, or document vault systems are fine; they know how to monitor and maintain what the company already has in the way of its Quality System. But if you're a medical device executive who is looking to design a structure that is efficient, compliant, scalable, and offers company-wide transparency, you're going to need a new architect—that's Consiliso. It contains the blueprints you need to design a Quality System that will take your company to the highest capabilities for continuous improvement.

> I have seen companies in the discovery stage of a lawsuit spend $100,000 on paralegals to do nothing more than search for documents and then create three pallets of copies. Why?

With Consiliso, companies that have in-house expertise on regulations can conduct their own assessment of their operations to begin implementation. That implementation then involves five phases: definition, requirements, integration, training, and auditing/reporting. It's an extensive but necessary change to the way your company operates if it wants to continue on a path of continuous growth, a path that may lead to the need for fewer audits and inspections in the near future.

Remember the "Maturity and Compliance Matrix," (Figure 1-1, in Chapter 1, "Consiliso: What It Is, What It Means to You")? Which quadrant of the matrix is your company in?

*Figure C-1: Maturity and Compliance Matrix*

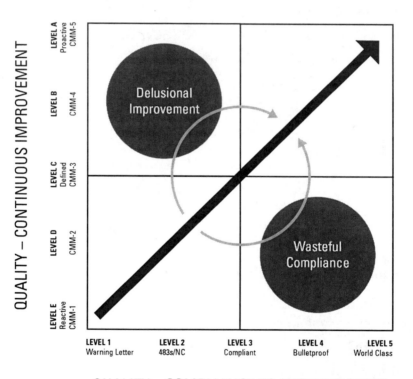

Consiliso breaks all the preconceived ideas for how to run a compliant medical device company. Consiliso provides a complete, detailed set of blueprints for every aspect (*what*, *why*, and *how*) of work within your company. It saves you time and money and gives an accurate picture of how your company operates.

Consiliso gives you an edge over your competition with its hyper-efficient methods of process re-use. And you do not need expensive software tools or a team of coders to implement and maintain your integrated business processes.

Hopefully, I made a compelling case for why Consiliso is the best way to build and grow your medical device company. I invite you to turn the page and learn more, contact the Consiliso team, and begin your journey to enjoying those short Quality System Management Reviews meetings I promised.

# LET'S TALK

Developing a complete blueprint to design and run your company with maximum efficiency and compliance can seem a daunting task, but you may already have many pieces in place.

Complete a simple assessment of your company at consiliso.com, and let us get in touch to discuss the many ways we can assist you. Mark is also available to speak to your company's leadership or at your quality or medical device industry event.

At Consiliso.com, you may also obtain a low-priced subscription to gain access to the latest Consiliso design information, as well as sample documents and templates to help you speed your implementation. We are also working closely with the Medical Device Innovation Consortium (MDIC.org) to ensure Consiliso concepts aid in raising the maturity level of your company, which the FDA has indicated could reduce your inspection burden.

You will also be able to purchase a discounted version of *Consiliso: The Blueprint for Integrating Business Processes in Medical Device Companies,* or access the textbook's chapters with your subscription.

**Visit us at www.consiliso.com**

**Or email us at info@consiliso.com**

CPSIA information can be obtained
at www.ICGtesting.com
Printed in the USA
FFOW04n2114101017

9 781599 328614